· PATHWAYS TO BLISS ·

OTHER TITLES IN
THE COLLECTED WORKS OF JOSEPH CAMPBELL

JOSEPH CAMPBELL

• PATHWAYS TO BLISS •

MYTHOLOGY
AND PERSONAL TRANSFORMATION

Edited and with a foreword by David Kudler

JOSEPH CAMPBELL FOUNDATION

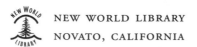
NEW WORLD LIBRARY
NOVATO, CALIFORNIA

New World Library
14 Pamaron Way
Novato, California 94949
www.newworldlibrary.com
1-800-972-6657

Cover design by Mary Ann Casler
Text design and typography by Tona Pearce Myers

Library of Congress Cataloging-in-Publication Data
Campbell, Joseph, 1904–1987
Pathways to bliss : mythology and personal transformation / Joseph Campbell ;
edited and with a foreword by David Kudler
    p.   m.
Includes bibliographical references and index.
ISBN-10: 1-57731-471-9 (hardcover : alk. paper)
ISBN-13: 978-1-57731-471-4
   1. Mythology—Psychological aspects. I. Kudler, David. II. Title.
BL315.C275 2004
201'.3019—dc22   2004014763

First printing, November 2004
ISBN-10: 1-57731-471-9
ISBN-13: 978-1-57731-471-4
Printed in Canada on acid-free, partially recycled paper

10 9 8 7

To know others is wisdom;
To know yourself is enlightenment
To master others requires force;
To master yourself requires true strength.

—Lao-tzu, *Tao-te Ching,* chapter 33

CONTENTS

ABOUT THE COLLECTED WORKS OF

JOSEPH CAMPBELL

At his death in 1987, Joseph Campbell left a significant body of published work that explored his lifelong passion, the complex of universal myths and symbols that he called "Mankind's one great story." He also left, however, a large volume of unreleased work: uncollected articles, notes, letters, and diaries, as well as audio- and videotape recorded lectures.

The Joseph Campbell Foundation was founded in 1991 to preserve, protect, and perpetuate Campbell's work. The Foundation has undertaken to archive his papers and recordings in digital format, and to publish previously unavailable material and out-of-print works as *The Collected Works of Joseph Campbell*.

THE COLLECTED WORKS OF JOSEPH CAMPBELL
Robert Walter, Executive Editor
David Kudler, Managing Editor

EDITOR'S FOREWORD

Joseph Campbell said in 1972, while he was compiling his book *Myths to Live By* from two decades' worth of lectures, that he experienced a revelation:

> My notion about myself was that I had grown up during that time, that my ideas had changed, and, too, that I had progressed. But when I brought these papers together, they were all saying essentially the same thing—over a span of decades. I found out something about the thing that was moving me. I didn't even have a very clear idea of what it was until I recognized those continuities running through that whole book. Twenty-four years is a pretty good stretch of time. A lot had happened during that period. And there I was babbling on about the same thing.[1]

As I compiled this book, which is drawn from over a dozen lectures, interviews, and seminars that Campbell gave between 1962 and 1983, I had a very similar impression.

I had culled all of these lectures because they traced Campbell's exploration of the idea of mythology as a tool for promoting and understanding the psychological growth of the individual—what he called the fourth or psychological function of myth. My first thought was to present a sort of historical overview of Campbell's thoughts on the subject.

And yet I found that the ideas that he was expostulating at the end of the period in which he was finishing his Cooper Union lectures and the gargantuan *Masks of God* series were indeed very much in line with those that he was continuing to explore close to the end of his life, albeit in more informal, intensive settings, such as the workshops at the Esalen Institute with which he celebrated his birthday every year. Some of his thinking grew—his feelings about the promise and dangers of LSD as a gateway to unlocking the mythic images of the collective unconscious, for example —yet the overall thesis remained the same. He felt that myth offered a framework for personal growth and transformation, and that understanding the ways that myths and symbols affect the individual mind offered a way to lead a life that was in tune with one's nature—a pathway to bliss.

The slow elaboration of his thoughts has made editing this volume both infinitely easier and infinitely more difficult than editing the previous volumes of *The Collected Works of Joseph Campbell* series that I have worked on. *Sake & Satori: Asian Journals—Japan* was drawn from a single, sequential source, which allowed me to concentrate on making sure that Campbell was telling his story well. *Myths of Light: Eastern Metaphors of the Eternal* was based on a number of lectures and unpublished writing, covering thirty years of Campbell's thinking on Indian and East Asian religion, but once I had sorted the topics into a form that made sense as an exploration of the idea of the transcendent divine, each section fell into place fairly cleanly, one lecture to a section.

The first section of the current volume, chapters 1 and 2, looks at the historical development of myth as a tool for the growth, not of societies, but of individuals. This section was drawn from a similarly diverse set of lectures; my main task in presenting them was to make sure that any redundancies were eliminated, so that the reader wasn't treated to four separate rehearsals of the four functions of mythology, for example.

The second section, however, chapters 3 through 5, focuses on the fundamental psychology of myth, and was drawn from a series of presentations delivered over the course of almost a decade, all entitled "Living Your Personal Myth" (a title which Campbell himself was never fully comfortable with). Sometimes this was an hour-long lecture, sometimes a week-long seminar. In each case, the topics covered shared a similar approach yet were presented in different order, with different emphasis, depending on Campbell's audience, then-current events, and his own developing thoughts on the subject. This made piecing together an intelligible but full exploration of his ideas more than usually challenging.

The third section, chapter 6, explores the basic premise set forth in Campbell's seminal work *The Hero with a Thousand Faces* as a tool for looking at one's own life. It presented yet another challenge. Most of this material was drawn from a three-day segment of a month-long seminar in 1983. Since the entire seminar took place in the form of an extremely free-form, wide-ranging discussion, its shape was extremely diffuse. Finding a narrative thread without either imposing a thesis or reducing the exploration to the point of incomprehensibility was challenging, to say the least. This was probably the most difficult, humbling experience of all.

One of the joys of reading—and editing—Joseph Campbell's work is that his mind, like Indra's net of gems, ties one glistening jewel of thought to another, always finding the connecting thread. As I said in the introduction to *Myths of Light*, the remarkable conceptual leaps in this volume you may attribute to Campbell. Any lapses of logic you may lay solely at my feet.

It is important to note that my contribution in bringing this book to life is but one of many. I would like to acknowledge the tireless work of JCF president Robert Walter, who has not only kept Campbell's legacy alive in the seventeen years since his death, who not only manages the small but thriving not-for-profit corporation that has kept Campbell's work moving forward, but who also helped me sort through crates of transcripts and audiotapes, drawing on his own experience as Campbell's friend and editor in searching for just the right material for this book.

I would also like to acknowledge the continued efforts of Jason Gardner of New World Library, who has been our partner in bringing this wonderful, growing series to life, and of Mike Ashby, who has barely broken a sweat when confronted by Sanskrit, Japanese, and *Finnegans Wake*.

I wish to acknowledge, too, the contributions of Sierra Millman and Shauna Shames, brilliant young people whom you will hear more of in years to come and who provided transcriptions for sections of this work. Ms. Millman additionally served as an early copyeditor for the first three chapters, which gave the current work its shape.

Finally, I wish to thank my wife, Maura Vaughn, with whom I tread the path, and who makes the path worth treading.

David Kudler

July 16, 2004

INTRODUCTION²

I was speaking to a group recently at the Esalen Institute in California. Most were women, and they were very interested in the question of whether there were role models to be found in classical myth for women trying to serve as soldiers and executives and such in modern life—which there weren't. And so the question came up of whether mythic figures should serve as role models at all.

I would say that, whether they should or shouldn't, the typical situation has been that a society's myths *do* provide role models for that society at that given time. What the mythic image shows is the way in which the cosmic energy manifests itself in time, and as the times change, the modes of manifestation change.

As I told them, the gods represent the patron powers that support you in your field of action. And by contemplating the deities, you're given a kind of steadying force that puts you in the role, as it were, that is represented by that particular deity. There are the patron deities of agriculture, patron deities of war, and so on. In our classical tradition, there is no patron deity for the woman in the field of business, action, warcraft, or so on. Athena is the patron of warriors, not a warrior herself. While Artemis may have been a huntress, what she represents is the transformative power of the goddess, of nature, not action within the social sphere. What could a businesswoman possibly learn from Artemis?

Where you have a mythic image, it has been validated by decades, centuries, or millennia of experience along that path, and it provides a model. It's not easy to build a life for yourself with no model whatsoever. I don't know how it is now, right this minute, when so many new possibilities have opened up for life. But in my experience it has always been the model that gives you the idea of the direction in which to go, and the way in which to handle the problems and opportunities that come up.

Myth is not the same as history; myths are not inspiring stories of people who lived notable lives. No, myth is the transcendent in relationship to the present. Now, a folk hero is different from the subject of a biography, even when the hero may have been a real person once upon a time—John Henry or George Washington. The folk hero represents a transforming feature in the myth. When you have an oral mythic tradition, it's right up to date. In the folktales of the American Indians, you have bicycles, you have the form of the Capitol dome in Washington. Everything gets incorporated into the mythology immediately. In our society of fixed texts and printed words, it is the function of the poet to see the life value of the facts round about, and to deify them, as it were, to provide images that relate the everyday to the eternal.

Of course, in trying to relate yourself to transcendence, you don't have to have images. You can go the Zen way and forget the myths altogether. But I'm talking about the mythic way. And what the myth does is to provide a field in which you can locate yourself. That's the sense of the mandala, the sacred circle, whether you are a Tibetan monk or the patient of a Jungian analyst. The symbols are laid out around the circle, and you are to locate yourself in the center. A labyrinth, of course, is a scrambled mandala, in which you don't know where you are. That's the way the world is for people who don't have a mythology. It's a labyrinth. They are battling their way through as if no one had ever been there before.

I've lately gotten to know the work of a splendid psychiatrist in Germany named Karlfried Graf Dürckheim (not to be confused with the French sociologist Émile Durkheim). This psychiatrist has summarized the whole problem of health—psychological and physical—with reference to myth, continuing the work of Carl Gustav Jung and Erich Neumann.³ There lives in us, says Dürckheim, a life wisdom. We are all manifestations of a mystic power: the power of life, which has shaped all life, and which has shaped us all in our mother's womb. And this kind of wisdom lives in us, and it represents the force of this power, this energy, pouring into the field of time and space. But it's a transcendent energy. It's an energy that comes from a realm beyond our powers of knowledge. And that energy becomes bound in each of us—in this body—to a certain commitment. Now, the mind that thinks, the eyes that see, they can become so involved in concepts and local, temporal tasks that we become bound up and don't let this energy flow through. And then we become sick. The energy is blocked, and we are thrown off center; this idea is very similar to the tenets of traditional Chinese and Indian medicine. So the psychological problem, the way to keep from becoming blocked, is to make yourself—and here is the phrase—*transparent to the transcendent.* It's as easy as that.

What myth does for you is to point beyond the phenomenal field toward the transcendent. A mythic figure is like the compass that you used to draw circles and arcs in school, with one leg in the field of time and the other in the eternal. The image of a god may look like a human or animal form, but its reference is transcendent of that.

Now, when you translate the moving, metaphoric foot of the compass into a concrete reference—into a fact—what you have is merely an allegory and not a myth. Where a myth points past itself to something indescribable, an allegory is merely a story or image that teaches a practical lesson. It is what Joyce would call *improper* art.⁴ If the reference of the mythic image is to a fact or to a concept, then you have an allegorical figure. A mythic figure has one leg in the transcendent. And one of the problems with the popularization of religious ideas is that the god becomes a final fact and is no longer itself transparent to the transcendent. This is what Lao-tzu means when he says, in the first aphorism of the *Tao-te Ching,* "The Tao that can be named is not the Tao."⁵

Make your god transparent to the transcendent, and it doesn't matter what his name is.

Now, when you have a deity as your model, your life becomes transparent to the transcendent, so far as you realize the inspiration of that god.

This means living, not in the name of success or achievement in the world, but rather in the name of transcendence, letting the energy come through.

Of course, to reach the transpersonal, you have to go through the personal; you have to have both qualities there. The nineteenth-century German ethnologist Adolf Bastian talked about there being two elements to every myth: the elementary and the local. You have to go through your own tradition—the local—to get to the transcendent, or elementary, level, and just so you have to have a relationship to God on both a personal and a transpersonal basis.

In primal societies, the shaman provides a living conduit between the local and the transcendent. The shaman is one who has actually gone through a psychological crack-up and recovery. The young boy or girl approaching adolescence either has a vision or hears a song. This vision or song amounts to a call. The person experiences a shivering, neurotic sickness. This is really a kind of psychotic episode, and the family, being in a tradition that knows about this thing, will send for a shaman to give the young person the disciplines that will carry them out of this dilemma. The disciplines include enacting certain psychological rites that put the individual back in touch with the society again, of singing his or her song.

Of course, what this individual has encountered by going deep into the unconscious is the unconscious of their whole society. These people are bound in a small horizon and share a limited system of psychological problems. And so the shaman becomes a teacher and a protector of the mythic tradition but is isolated and feared; it's a very dangerous position to be in.

Now, an older person can *want* to become a shaman in some societies, and so then has to undergo certain ordeals to gain the power that the primary shaman has gained automatically. In northeast Siberia and in many parts of North and South America, the call of the shaman involves a transvestite life. That is, the person is to live the life of the opposite sex. What this means is that the person has transcended the powers of his or her original gender, and so women live as men and men live as women. These transvestite shamans play a very large role in the Indian mythology in the Southwest—the Hopi, the Pueblo, the Navaho, and the Apache—and also among the Sioux Indians and many others.

Waldemar Bogoras and Waldemar Jochelson first recognized this gender reversal among the Chukchi people on the Kamchatka Peninsula in Siberia.[6] These two men witnessed a constellation of reactions to this phenomenon. One is that some young men who had heard the call to become what they call a "soft man" were so ashamed and so negative to it that they committed suicide. If the shaman does not answer the call, then he will be psychologically shipwrecked and will fall to pieces. It's a very deep psychological summons.

I recently read the story of a woman who grew up in a mining town in West Virginia. When she was a little girl, she went walking in the woods and heard marvelous music. And she didn't know what to do with it, or anything about it. The years passed her by, and, in her sixties, she came to a psychiatrist with the feeling that she had missed a life. It was in deep, hypnotic memories she recalled this song.[7] You recognize it, of course: it's the shaman's song.

It is through attending to this song, to this visionary image, that the shamans center themselves. They give themselves peace by chanting the songs and performing the rites. At the very tip of South America, in Tierra del Fuego, there live about the simplest tribal people on the American continent, the Ona and Yagan people. In the early twentieth century, Father Alberto de Agostini, a priest who was also a scientist, lived among them for some time and gave us practically all we know about their mythology. He tells of waking up in the night and hearing the local shaman playing his drum and chanting his song alone, all night long—holding himself to the power.[8]

Now, that idea of holding yourself to the power by way of your dream myth is indicative of the way in which myth works generally. If it is a living mythology, one that is actually organically relevant to the life of the people of the time, repeating the myths and enacting the rituals center you. Ritual is simply myth enacted; by participating in a rite, you are participating directly in the myth.

In the Navaho world today, where there is a great deal of neurosis because these warrior people are on a reservation rather than leading their traditional lives, the sand-painting rituals are used for healing—just going over the myth and over the myth. This makes you transparent to the transcendent.

This is the way myth works.

I find, in my experience of these matters, that my best teaching has always come from India. Back when I was about to turn fifty and had been studying and teaching mythology for half a lifetime, I finally asked myself, How do I pull all this together? Well, I thought, there's one place where myth has been dominant for ages, and not only dominant but translated into ideas, so that you can read about it; there are millennia's worth of commentary and discussion. You aren't forced simply to get what you can from immediate aesthetic appreciation.

So I went to India, and suddenly everything made sense to me.[9] I have found my own best thinking in these matters comes largely out of what I learned from there.

There is a doctrine that comes out of the Vedantic tradition that has helped me to understand the nature of the energy that flows through myths. The Taittirīya Upaniṣad speaks of five sheaths that enclose the *ātman,* which is the spiritual ground or germ of the individual.

The first sheath is called *annamaya-kośa,* the food sheath. That is your body, which is made out of food and which will become food when you die. The worms, the vultures, the hyenas, or the flame will consume it. This is the sheath of our physical body: the food sheath.

The second sheath is called the sheath of breath, *prānamaya-kośa.* The breath oxidizes the food; the breath turns it into *life.* That's this thing, this body: food on fire.

The next sheath is called the mental sheath, *manomaya-kośa.* This is the consciousness of the body, and it coordinates the senses with the you that thinks it is you.

Then there is a big gap.

And the next sheath is called the wisdom sheath, *vijñānamaya-kośa.* This is the sheath of the wisdom of the transcendent pouring in. This is the wisdom that brought you to form in the mother womb, that digests your dinners, that knows how to do it. This is the wisdom that, when you cut yourself, knows how to heal the wound. The cut bleeds, and then a scab comes along; finally a scar forms, and this is the wisdom sheath going to work.

You go for a walk in the woods. Somebody has built a barbed-wire fence. It leans right into the tree. The tree incorporates that barbed wire. The tree has it, the wisdom sheath. This is the level of your nature wisdom that you share with the hills, with the trees, with the fish, with the animals. The power of myth is to put the mental sheath in touch with this wisdom sheath, which is the one that speaks of the transcendent.

And the sheath inward of the wisdom sheath is the sheath of bliss, *ānandamaya-kośa*, which is a kernel of that transcendence in and of itself. Life is a manifestation of bliss. But *manomaya-kośa*, the mental sheath, is attached to the sufferings and pleasures of the food sheath. And so it thinks, Is life worth living? Or, as Joyce asks in *Finnegans Wake*, "Was liffe worth leaving?"[10]

Just think: the grass grows. Out of the bliss sheath comes the wisdom sheath and the grass grows. Then, every two weeks, someone comes along with a lawn mower and cuts the grass down. Suppose the grass were just to think, Ah, shucks, what's all this fuss about? I quit?

That's mental sheath stuff. You know that impulse: life is painful; how could a good god create a world with all of this in it? That is thinking in terms of good and evil, light and dark—pairs of opposites. The wisdom sheath doesn't know about pairs of opposites. The bliss sheath contains all opposites. The wisdom sheath is just coming right up out of it, and it turns into pairs of opposites later on.

When I was in Egypt, I went to the miserable little tomb of Tutankhamen. Compared with the tomb of Seti I right beside it, it was just somebody's outhouse. There are two little rooms the size of a studio apartment. Seti's tomb is as big as a small gymnasium. That's why nobody bothered to rifle Tutankhamen's tomb, and that's why we got all that wonderful stuff from it.

Think about the coffin of Tutankhamen in terms of the Indian image of the sheaths. I don't know if that is what the Egyptian sculptors intended, but this is what I saw. You have three quadrangular boxes, one inside the other: food sheath, breath sheath, and mental sheath. That's the outside. Then you have a great stone coffin that separates the inner two sheaths from the ones on the outside. And what do you have inside? You have a sarcophagus made of wood, inlaid with gold and lapis lazuli. This is shaped in the form of the young king, with his signs of kingship crossed over his chest. That, I would say, is the wisdom sheath, the level of the living organic form.

And within that is the sheath of bliss: a solid gold coffin in the form of Tutankhamen, with several tons of gold. When you realize how gold was mined in those days, that sarcophagus cost many a life and lots of suffering to get that much gold. And this was the sheath of bliss.

And within this, of course, was the *ātman,* the body itself. Unfortunately, the Egyptians made the enormous error of mistaking eternal life for the eternal concretized life of the body. And so what do you find when you go to the Egyptian Museum? You pay an extra dollar to go to the Mummy Room. And you come into a room with three rows of wooden coffins. And in each sleeps a pharaoh. And the names of the pharaohs are there like the names on a collection of butterflies: Amenhotep I, II, III, and so forth.

All I could think of was the room in a maternity ward, the nursery where they have the little babies. The Egyptians based all of this—building the pyramids and these great tombs—on this basic mistake, that eternal life is the life of *annamaya-kośa,* the food sheath. It has nothing to do with any such thing. Eternity has nothing to do with time. Time is what shuts you out from eternity. Eternity is now. It is the transcendent dimension of the now to which myth refers.

All of these things enable you to understand what myth really is about. When people say, "Well, you know, this couldn't have happened, and that couldn't have happened, and so let's get rid of the myths," what they are doing is getting rid of the vocabulary of discourse between *manomaya-kośa* and *vijñānamaya-kośa,* between mental wisdom and organic, life-body wisdom.

These deities in myths serve as models, give you life roles, so long as you understand their reference to the foot in the transcendent. The Christian idea of *Imitatio Christi,* the imitation of Christ—what does that mean, that you should go out and get yourself crucified? Nothing of the kind. It means to live with one foot in the transcendent, as God.

As Paul says, "I live; yet not I, but Christ liveth in me."[11] That means that the eternal thing works in me. And this is the meaning of the Buddha consciousness, the consciousness that is both the entire universe and you yourself.

The myths tells you that if you engage the world in a certain way, you are under the protection of Athena, under the protection of Artemis, under the protection of this, that, or the other god. That's the model. We don't have that today. Life has changed in form so rapidly that even the forms that were normal to think about in the time of my boyhood are no longer around, and there's another set, and everything is moving very, very fast. Today we don't have the stasis that is required for the formation of a mythic tradition.

The rolling stone gathers no moss. Myth is moss. So now you've got to do it yourself, ad lib. I speak of the present as a moment of free fall into the future with no guidance. All you've got to know is how to fall; and you can learn that, too. That is the situation with regard to myth right now. We're all without dependable guides.

Yet even now you can find two guides. The first can be a personality in your youth who seemed to you a noble and great personality. You can use that person as a model. The other way is to live for bliss. In this way, your bliss becomes your life. There's a saying in Sanskrit: the three aspects of thought that point furthest toward the border of the abyss of the transcendent are *sat, cit,* and *ānanda:* being, consciousness, and bliss.[12] You can call transcendence a hole or the whole, either one, because it is beyond words. All that we can talk about is what is on this side of transcendence. And the problem is to open the words, to open the images so that they point past themselves. They will tend to shut off the experience through their own opacity. But these three concepts are those that will bring you closest to that void: *sat-cit-ānanda.* Being, consciousness, and bliss.

Now, as I've gotten older, I've been thinking about these things. And I don't know what being is. And I don't know what *consciousness* is. But I do know what *bliss* is: that deep sense of being present, of doing what you absolutely must do to be yourself. If you can hang on to that, you are on the edge of the transcendent already. You may not have any money, but it doesn't matter. When I came back from my student years in Germany and Paris, it was three weeks before the Wall Street crash in 1929, and I didn't have a job for five years. And, fortunately for me, there was no welfare. I had nothing to do but sit in Woodstock and read and figure out where my bliss lay. There I was, on the edge of excitement all the time.

So, what I've told my students is this: follow your bliss. You'll have moments when you'll experience bliss. And when that goes away, what happens to it? Just stay with it, and there's more security in that than in finding out where the money is going to come from next year. For years I've watched this whole business of young people deciding on their careers. There are only two attitudes: one is to follow your bliss; and the other is to read the projections as to where the money is going to be when you graduate. Well, it changes so fast. This year it's computer work; next year it's dentistry, and so on. And no matter what the young person decides, by the time he or she gets going, it will have changed. But if they have found where the center of their real bliss is, they can have that. You may not have money, but you'll have your bliss.

Your bliss can guide you to that transcendent mystery, because bliss is the welling up of the energy of the transcendent wisdom within you. So when the bliss cuts off, you know that you've cut off the welling up; try to find it again. And that will be your Hermes guide, the dog that can follow the invisible trail for you. And that's the way it is. One works out one's own myth that way.

You can get some clues from earlier traditions. But they have to be taken as clues. As many a wise man has said, "You can't wear another person's hat." So when people get excited about the Orient and begin putting on turbans and saris, what they've gotten caught in is the folk aspect of the wisdom that they need. You've got to find the wisdom, not the clothing of it. Through those trappings, the myths of other cultures, you can come to a wisdom that you've then got to translate into your own. The whole problem is to turn these mythologies into your own.

Now, in my courses in mythology at Sarah Lawrence, I taught people of practically every religious faith you could think of. Some have a harder time mythologizing than others, but all have been brought up in a myth of some kind. What I've found is that any mythic tradition can be translated into your life, if it's been put into you. And it's a good thing to hang on to the myth that was put in when you were a child, because it is there whether you want it there or not. What you have to do is translate that myth into its eloquence, not just into the literacy. You have to learn to hear its song.

I have a friend—a very interesting chap—who started out as a Presbyterian, got interested in Hinduism, and then served as an acolyte to a Hindu monk in New York for twenty years or so. Then he went to India and became a Hindu monk himself. One day he phones me and says, "Joe, I'm going to become a Catholic."[13]

Well, the Church has become interested in ecumenical totality. At least, they think they are. Of course, when you sit down at the table with them, they're not interested in that at all. They're holding the cards very close. They handle it by knocking down the other systems. My friend, who has now gone from being a Hindu monk to a Roman Catholic, has been writing for an American Jesuit magazine, and he said, "No, you can't treat other religions that way. If you're going to get in touch with what the Hindus or Buddhists are thinking about, you have to find out what they're thinking about, and not just read it in a derogatory way."

And so he was sent over to Bangkok at the time of a great meeting of the monastic orders of the Catholic tradition. That was the conference where Thomas Merton was killed by a bad electrical fixture in some Bangkok hotel.

The interesting thing that my friend told me was that the Roman Catholic monks and the Buddhist monks had no trouble understanding each other. Each of them was seeking the same experience and knew that the experience was incommunicable. The communication is only an effort to bring the hearer to the edge of the abyss; it is a signpost, not the thing itself. But the secular clergy reads the communication and gets stuck with the letter, and that's where you have the conflict.

My old mentor, Heinrich Zimmer, had a little saying: the best things can't be told—they are transcendent, inexpressible truths. The second-best are misunderstood: myths, which are metaphoric attempts to point the way toward the first. And the third-best have to do with history, science, biography, and so on. The only kind of talking that can be understood is this last kind. When you want to talk about the first kind, that which can't be said, you use the third kind as communication to the first. But people read it as referring to the third directly; the image is no longer transparent to the transcendent.

Here is a story that seems to me to embody the essential image of living one's life, finding it and having the courage to pursue it. It comes from an

Arthurian romance, *La Queste del Saint Graal,* by an anonymous thirteenth-century monk.

There's a moment there in Arthur's banquet hall when all the knights are assembled around the Round Table. Arthur would not let anyone start to eat until an adventure had occurred. Well, in those days adventures were rather normal, so people didn't go hungry for long.

They were waiting for this day's adventure, and it did indeed occur. The Holy Grail itself showed itself to the assembled knights—not in its full glory but covered with a great, radiant cloth. Then it withdrew. All were left ravished, sitting there in awe.

Finally, Gawain, Arthur's nephew, stood up and said, "I propose a vow to this company, that we should all go in quest of that Grail to behold it unveiled."

Now we come to the text that interested me. The text reads, "They thought it would be a disgrace to go forth in a group. Each entered the Forest Adventurous at that point which he himself had chosen, where it was darkest and there was no way or path."

You enter the forest at the darkest point, where there is no path. Where there's a way or path, it is someone else's path; each human being is a unique phenomenon.

The idea is to find your own pathway to bliss.

CHAPTER I

THE NECESSITY OF RITES[14]

THE FUNCTIONS OF MYTHOLOGY

Traditionally, the first function of a living mythology is to reconcile consciousness to the preconditions of its own existence; that is to say, to the nature of life.

Now, life lives on life. Its first law is, now I'll eat you, now you eat me—quite something for consciousness to assimilate. This business of life living on life—on death—had been in process for billions of years before eyes opened and became aware of what was going on out there, long before *Homo sapiens*'s appearance in the universe. The organs of life had evolved to depend on the death of others for their existence. These organs have impulses of which your consciousness isn't even aware; when it becomes aware of them, you may become scared that this eat-or-be-eaten horror is what you are.

The impact of this horror on a sensitive consciousness is terrific—this monster which is life. Life is a horrendous presence, and you wouldn't be here if it weren't for that. The first function of a mythological order has been to reconcile consciousness to this fact.

The first, primitive orders of mythology are affirmative: they embrace life on its own terms. I don't think any anthropologist could document a primitive mythology that was world-negating. When you realize what primitive people run up against—the pains and the agonies and the problems simply of existing—I think it's quite amazing. I've studied a lot of the myths of these cultures around the world, and I can't recall a single negative word in primitive thought with respect to existence or to the universe. World-weariness comes later, with people who are living high on the hog.

The only way to affirm life is to affirm it to the root, to the rotten, horrendous base. It is this kind of affirmation that one finds in the primitive rites. Some of these rites are so brutal you can hardly read about, let alone look at, them. Yet they present a vivid image before the young adolescent mind: life is a monstrous thing, and if you're going to live, you've got to live *this* way; which is to say, within the traditions of the tribe.

That's the first function of mythology: not merely a reconciliation of consciousness to the preconditions of its own existence, but reconciliation with gratitude, with love, with recognition of the sweetness. Through the bitterness and pain, the primary experience at the core of life is a sweet, wonderful thing. This affirmative view comes pouring in on one through these terrific rites and myths.

Then, in about the eighth century B.C., there came what I call the Great Reversal. People of a certain sensitivity and sensibility found that they could not affirm the daily horror of life. Their worldview echoes in the words of Schopenhauer: "Life is something that should not have been."[15] Life is a fundamental, metaphysical, cosmic mistake. Many found it so horrible that they retreated from it.

What, then, is the mythology that emerges? At that time, there came into being mythologies of retreat, dismissal, renunciation—life denial. Here we find the mythological orders of escape. And I mean real escape: getting out of the world. Yet how can you go about canceling in yourself either the urge to live on or the resentment that life doesn't give you what you think it ought to give you, that it turns out to be this horror? How can you quench the life urge or the life disappointment? By honoring the world-negating, cosmos-negating mythologies that serve this function. Jainism or early monastic Buddhism would be prime examples of this metaphysical approach.

Jainism is perhaps the oldest functioning religion in the world. A very small number of Jains still live, principally in and around Bombay. And their first law is *ahiṃsā,* nonviolence, not hurting any life. Ironically, they are an enormously wealthy group in India because, if you want to take a career that would not injure life—at least physically—banking turns out to be one of the best. So they have become a very small but extremely elite group.

Like most negative sects, they fall into two communities. One is the lay community, the members who still live in the world. And the other community is made up of the monks and nuns who are supported by the community. Finally, of course, they don't need much support at all because they go into the forest and their main job is to *get out.*

How do you go about that? You start by giving up eating anything that seems to be alive. You won't, of course, eat meat; that's taboo number 1. But you won't even eat what seems to be a live vegetable. You wouldn't pick an orange or an apple. You would wait for it to fall. Imagine how delightful the gourmet table of a Jain ascetic would be. Finally, it gets down to eating only dead leaves and things like that, but you learn by yogic breathing and discipline to digest every little particle of every little thing you eat.

The second aim is, through this kind of living, to lose all desire for life. The idea is not to die before you have lost all desire for life, to make these two coincide. In the ultimate stages, you are to take a vow each day not to take more than a certain number of steps; you will reduce the number of steps over time because every time you step, particularly in the forest, you are hurting the fungi, the ants, perhaps even the soil.

The idea in this tradition—and it's a fantastic image of the universe—is that all things are living souls, what can be called monads of life, on the way up. What you are stepping on is alive. And through a great number of incarnations, it will have reached a life as a human, which will be stepping on something that is alive. I think it's one of the grandest images of the whole universe: the rising pool of *jīvas,* or living monads. It makes me think of a pop bottle when you take the top off—all the bubbles coming up. Where do they come from? Where do they go? They come from beyond all categories, and they go beyond all categories. But meanwhile, in life, they're on the way up.

So here we have two attitudes toward the great mystery. One is of complete affirmation. You don't say no to anything. You can control your existence and your system of values and your social role and so on, but in your heart and in your depth, you are saying yes to it all. The other is indeed saying no—all the way, too. And you don't participate in the horror of it all any more than you have to. Your whole game is to get out.

A third system emerges, as far as the documents tell, in Zoroastrianism, which dates from between the eleventh and perhaps the seventh centuries B.C. The notion appears of a deity—Ahura Mazda, the lord of light and truth—who created a perfect world. Angra Mainyu, the lord of deception, destroys or negates this world. According to Zarathustra (or Zoroaster), a restoration of the perfect world is under way, and we can participate in that restoration. By favoring the good against the evil in our lives and deeds, we will gradually help restore the lost good world.

You will recognize this belief form as something that has come to us by way of the late stages in the biblical tradition and in the Christian tradition of the Fall and the Resurrection.

This third position, then, offers an ameliorative mythology. This worldview expresses the notion that through certain kinds of activity, a change can be brought about. Through prayer or good deeds or some other activity, one can change the basic principles, the fundamental preconditions of life. You affirm the world on condition that it follows your notion of what the world should be. This is like marrying someone in order to improve him or her—it is not marriage.

These are, as far as I know, the three main mythological points of view in the high cultures: one is altogether affirming, another altogether rejecting, and a third says, "I will affirm the world when it gets to be the way I think it should be." The popular secularization of this last position finds voice, of course, in the progressive, world-reforming attitude that we recognize around us.

A mythological order is a system of images that gives consciousness a sense of meaning in existence, which, my dear friend, has no meaning— it simply is. But the mind goes asking for meanings; it can't play unless it knows (or makes up) some system of rules.

Mythologies present games to play: how to make believe you're doing thus and so. Ultimately, through the game, you experience that positive thing which is the experience of being-in-being, of living meaningfully. That's the first function of mythology, to evoke in the individual a sense of grateful, affirmative awe before the monstrous mystery that is existence.

The second function of mythology is to present an image of the cosmos, an image of the universe round about, that will maintain and elicit this experience of awe. This function we may call the cosmological function of mythology.

The question of truth doesn't matter here. Nietzsche says that the worst point you can present to a person of faith is truth. Is it true? Who cares? In the sphere of mythological imagery, the point is, I like it this way; this is the source of my life. Question the cosmological authenticity of a clergyman's archaic image of the universe, his notion of the history of the world—"Who are you, pride of intellect, to question this wonderful thing that's been the source of all my life?"

People live by playing a game, and you can ruin a game by being Sir Sobersides who comes in and says, "Well, what's the use of this?" A cosmological image gives you a field in which to play the game that helps you to reconcile your life, your existence, to your own consciousness, or expectation, of meaning. This is what a mythology or a religion has to offer.

Of course, the system must make sense. One of the most bewildering experiences I ever had was during the *Apollo 10* Moon flight. This was the one just before the actual moon landing, when these three wonderful men were flying around the Moon just at Christmas. They were talking about how dry and barren the Moon looked. And then, in honor of the holiday, they began reading from the first Book of Genesis. Here they were, reading these ancient words that had nothing to do with the cosmos they were flying through, describing a flat three-layer cake of a universe that had been created in seven days by a God who lived somewhere below the sphere that they were in at the time. They talked about the separating of the waters above and the waters below, when they had just pointed out how dry it was. The whole discontinuity between the religious tradition and the actual physical condition struck me very strongly that evening. What a calamity for our world that we do not yet have anything that can wake people's hearts the way that those verses do and yet would make sense in terms of the actual, observable universe!

One of the problems in our biblical tradition is that the universe presented is one posited by the Sumerians five thousand years ago; we've had two universe models since then. There's been the Ptolemaic system, and, for the past four or five hundred years, we've had the Copernican universe, with the solar system and the wheeling galaxies. But here we are, stuck with that funny little story in the first chapter of Genesis. This doesn't have anything to do with any of the rest, not even the second chapter of Genesis.

The second function of mythology, then, is to present an image of the cosmos that will maintain your sense of mystical awe and explain everything that you come into contact with in the universe around you.

The third function of a mythological order is to validate and maintain a certain sociological system: a shared set of rights and wrongs, proprieties or improprieties, on which your particular social unit depends for its existence.

In the traditional societies, these notions of order and law are held in the frame of the cosmological order: they are of the same essential nature, equally valid and equally unquestionable. In the biblical tradition, for example, you find a single God who created the universe; that same deity is supposed to have announced the social laws to Moses on Mount Sinai, the Ten Commandments, and so forth. So, the social laws of this holy society have the same authenticity as the laws of the universe. You can't say, "Oh, gosh, I don't like it that the sun rises so early in the springtime and summertime. I'd rather have it arrive later." Neither can you say, "Oh, I don't like it that one cannot eat meat and milk at the same meal." Both laws come down from the same source. They are apodictic; that is to say, they cannot be denied. The social orders of a traditional, myth-based society are as authentic and as far beyond criticism as the laws of the universe itself. You cannot change these; you cannot go against them except to your own destruction.

This is characteristic of the old traditional mythological notions of morality. The morality is given, and no human congress can decide, "This is now out of date, this is now absurd, this is now something that's going to knock us all to pieces. Let's change it. Let's be rational about this thing." The Church can't do anything about that, and no traditional society can do anything about it. This is the law, and that's that. The Pope is facing this with his problem with contraception. He's in an absurd position, saying that he somehow knows what God has to say about these things.

I just have a little message for the Pope, and I haven't been able to get it to him, but when Dante, in *The Divine Comedy,* gets to the heavenly auditorium of the heavenly rose, Beatrice points the congregation out to him. They see this glorious white rose, with the Trinity in the middle. Let's call it the Rose Bowl. And it's got a multitude of people, all the souls that have been created to fill the place of the angels that fell. Beatrice points out to Dante that it's almost full. Now that was in 1300, and think what's happened since. The Pope just hasn't read his books correctly. It's time to stop this thing, you see. It's already been delivered, the message has. So at a certain point you need to quit filling up that bowl. There's not even standing room. In any case, so it is in the biblical tradition.

You find something like this in India, where you have the idea, not of a creator god, but of *brahman,* an impersonal power that brings the universe into being and takes it away again. Part and parcel of this universal order are the laws that govern the different species of animals and plants, as well as the laws of the Indian social order, the caste system. These cannot be changed. They are an expression of the universal order.

Now, in India to this day there is a conflict between the tradition of caste and of the taboos that come from that tradition on the one hand, and the secular law of the present state of India on the other. A few years ago the high priest at one of the great Hindu temples said, "If you want to be British, break caste. If you want to be Hindu, obey the scriptures." And the scriptures tell that each caste has its proper function and place. So, in the traditional society, the social order is part of the natural order, and there is such a thing as a moral law. People still use this term, but what was moral yesterday can become vice today. It certainly can, and it has so become; I have watched this in my lifetime.

Finally, the fourth function of mythology is psychological. The myth must carry the individual through the stages of his life, from birth through maturity through senility to death. The mythology must do so in accord with the social order of his group, the cosmos as understood by his group, and the monstrous mystery.

The second and third functions have been taken over in our world by secular orders. Our cosmology is in the hands of science. The first law of science is that the truth has not been found. The laws of science are working hypotheses. The scientist knows that at any moment facts may be found that make the present theory obsolete; this is happening now constantly. It's amusing. In a religious tradition, the older the doctrine, the truer it is held to be.

In the scientific tradition, on the other hand, a paper written ten years ago is already out of date. There's a continuous movement onward. So there's no law, no Rock of Ages on which you can rest. There's nothing of the kind. It's fluid. And we know that rocks are fluid, too, though it takes them a long time to flow. Nothing lasts. It all changes.

In the social realm, again, we don't regard our laws as being divinely ordained. You still hear it from time to time, as in the current abortion problem: God is talking to Senator So-and-so, or Reverend Thus-and-such. But it doesn't seem to make sense otherwise. God's law is no longer the justification for the nation's laws. Congress decides what a decent aim for the social order is and what the institution is that should bring that aim about. So I would say that in this secular society of ours, we can no longer really think of the cosmological and sociological functions as a problem.

However, in all of our lives, the first and fourth functions do still play a role, and it's these that I will be addressing. We are going to find ourselves far away from the old traditions. The first is the problem of awe. And, as I've said, you can have one of three attitudes toward it.

The fourth function now is the pedagogical. Basically, the function of the pedagogical order is to bring a child to maturity and then to help the aged become disengaged. Infancy is a period of obedience and dependency. The child is dependent on the parent, looks to the parent for advice and help and approval. There comes a time, however, when the individual has to become self-reliant and not dependent but himself the authority. Now here we come to a distinction between the traditional attitude toward this problem and the contemporary Western one. The traditional idea is that the adult who has moved from dependency to responsibility should take over without criticism the laws of the society and represent them. In our world, we ask for the development of the individual's critical faculties, that you should evaluate the social order and yourself, then contribute criticism. This doesn't mean blowing it up. Nor does it mean blowing it up before you've found out what it is.

I want to speak about this last function at greater length.

Myth and the Development of the Individual

I find that the psychological is the most constant of the four functions across cultures. Just consider the problem of a developing individual, whether a Sioux on the eighteenth-century plains of North America, a Congolese in the ancient jungles of Africa, or a contemporary urbanite in this wild, mechanically constructed environment that we modern folk find ourselves in today. We all follow a very similar path, in terms of our psychological development, from the cradle to the grave.

The first fact that distinguishes the human species from all others is that we are born too soon. We arrive, incapable of taking care of ourselves for something like fifteen years. Puberty doesn't come along for twelve years or more, and physical maturity doesn't arrive until our early twenties. During the greater part of this long arc of life, the individual is in a psychological situation of dependency. We are trained, as children, so that every stimulus, every experience, leads us simply to react, "Who will help me?" We are in a dependent relationship to our parents. Every situation evokes parental images: "What would Mommy and Daddy want me to do?" Freud made a great point of this dependence.

If you go for a PhD, for example, you're not going to get out from under the authorities until you're perhaps forty-five years old. But then you'll never get out. You can always tell an author who is still working under the authorities by the number of footnotes he provides to his text. You must have the courage of your own belief and leave it to somebody else to verify your authority for him- or herself.

Now compare, for instance, a professor talking on the television, answering questions, with an athlete being interviewed. The academic will very often hem and haw, and you'll wonder, Does he actually have an idea? What's stopping him? Then you watch the baseball player, and he responds easily. He speaks with authority. He speaks with ease. I've always been impressed by this. That athlete got out from under the authorities when he was the best pitcher in the sandlot at the age of seventeen or eighteen. The poor professor was working under the authorities until he was turning gray, and now it's just too late. Now it's time for him to go out the door entirely.

At a certain point in life, society asks this dependent little creature to become a responsible initiator of action, one who doesn't simply turn for help to Daddy or Mommy but *is* Daddy or Mommy.

The function of the puberty rites in cultures older than our own was to effect a psychological transformation, and it doesn't matter whether you can add 2 + 2 or 962,000 + x. The main thing is that you assume responsibility in a snap, without correcting yourself. The person who is torn between attitudes of dependency and of responsibility is the neurotic: he is ambivalent, pulled in two directions.

Neurotics are simply people who have not crossed the psychological threshold completely. They have an experience, and the first response is, "Where's Daddy?" Then suddenly the realization comes: "Oh, I'm Daddy!" These forty-year-old infants, weeping on a Freudian couch, are simply people who first react dependently and then have to think, "Oh, wait a sec, I've grown up."

So, everyone is raised with an attitude of submission to authority and fear of punishment: always looking to those above you for approval or disapproval. Then, suddenly, at puberty, you are supposed to become an adult and take responsibility for your own life. All the automatic responses that, for something like twenty years, have triggered submission to authority are supposed to give way to an assumption of authority for yourself. The primitive initiation and puberty rites, which survive in the little slap the bishop is supposed to give at confirmation, are to *wake you up;* wake up your adulthood, leave your childhood behind.

Among the aboriginal Aranda people in Australia, for example, when little boys begin to become nasty and difficult for their mothers to handle, the women get together and give them a good beating around the legs with sticks and so forth. Then, in a few weeks, something very interesting happens. The men, all dressed in strange godlike costumes such as the youngsters have always been taught were the figures of the divinities, come in with bull-roarers and yawls and all kinds of terrifying noisemakers. The boys run to their mothers for protection. And the mothers pretend to protect them. Then the men grab them and take them away, so Mother's no good anymore; now they have to face this thing.

And what they have to face is really no fun. One of the little crises takes place when the men place the boys behind a screen of bushes. A lot of very interesting things are going on outside at night—dances and so forth. The boys are told not to look. Well, can you imagine what's done with any boy who does look? He's killed and eaten.

That is certainly one way to handle juvenile delinquents. Simply eradicate any youngster who will not cooperate with the society that is supporting him. Of course, the bad part of this method is that it deprives the community of original talents: only the good boys survive.

After a while, each boy is given a chance to see what is going on out there. So he takes a seat beyond the screen, a scared kid, about twelve or thirteen years old. At the end of this dance field, a strange man comes out, performing the myth of the Cosmic Kangaroo. Then the Cosmic Dog comes out and attacks the Kangaroo. This performance is all part of the mythology of the totem ancestor. So the youngster is sitting on the edge, watching the show, when these two big fellows come rushing down the field and jump on him. And continue to jump on him.

Well, now he is going to remember Kangaroo and Dog forever. It may not be terribly sophisticated, but the boy gets the point, and there are not many points to be got. All the early images of the father and the mother are transferred to the ancestral images of the tribe itself.

A series of other pretty exciting things happen: there are more pageants, and the boy is circumcised. He is given a special little thing called a *tjurunga,* which is supposed to heal the wound and protect him and become his sort of personal fetish and so forth. The men feed the boy on their own blood. They cut arms and so forth, and the kid lives on blood: cakes of blood, blood soup—blood is poured all over him.

When it's all over, the kid isn't the kid he was before the ritual. A lot has happened. His body has been changed, his psyche has changed, and then he's sent back to the girls.

And there one of them is, the daughter of the man who circumcised the boy, already selected to be his wife. He has no choice; there's no personal discretion here. He has no chance to say, "I don't like this. I want something else." Now he's a guaranteed little man, and he's going to behave as a man of this crowd ought to behave.[16]

These societies are up against a survival problem, and the individual who is initiated into the social order must be initiated in such a way that his spontaneous responses will be in accord with the needs of that society. The society shapes him to order: he's being trimmed and cut into being an organ of a certain organism. No independent thoughts, please.

In the societies of a traditional culture, then, maturity is the condition of living within the bounds of the cultural traditions. You become the vehicle of the moral order. You enforce it. You believe it. You are it.

In our culture, we have a different requirement. We ask our students, our children, to be critical, to use their heads, to become individuals, and to assume responsibility for their own lives. Some of them start too soon, it seems to me, but on the whole this is a principle of great creative potency. Yet it leads to a very new problem in relation to our mythologies. Unlike traditional cultures, we do not try to imprint the tradition onto the person with such force that the individual becomes simply a walking copy of what was there before. Rather, the idea is to develop the individual personality—a special and contemporary Western problem, it may surprise you to learn.

In India, for example, the individual is expected to do exactly as has traditionally been expected of a person of his caste. That old ritual of *satī*—the woman throwing herself on her husband's funeral pyre, the rite so abhorrent to our sensibilities—is from a Sanskrit word, *sat,* which is the feminine form of the verb meaning "to be." A woman who performs her duty all the way as wife *is* something, precisely because she is a wife. And the person who disobeys this *sat,* this dharma, this supporting law, is *asat:* a "no thing."

This point of view is just the opposite of our Western point of view. If a person simply lives by authority and does exactly as told, identifying himself with his social role, we would call him a square, a fuddy-duddy— "There is no person there."

Next we come to a psychological transformation that all people have had to face: the transit from maturity to senility and failing powers. In primitive societies and all of the archaic high cultures, this transition comes earlier than it does for us, with our highly developed medical profession; in many societies, it's astonishing how early this old-age crisis begins to move in. At any rate, no matter when it comes, it comes.

Just about when you've learned what your instructors have told you to learn, suppressing all of the movements of the spirit that are incompatible with your local social order, just about the time when you begin to be informed, to govern and direct, you begin to lose your grip. The mind fails to remember things, the hands drop things, you find yourself more tired than you used to be at the end of the day, sleep becomes a much more congenial thought than action—you're beginning to drop out. Furthermore, another very vigorous generation with a different hairdo has come along, and you think, Well, let them have it. The mythologies have to take care of this dropout situation.

When all the energies of your life and all the energies that the world has asked for have been applied to the aims of a given social order and then you find these aims either changed or no longer susceptible to your actions, you fall into a psychological tailspin. The energies of the psyche fall back into those realms of the depths of being that the society didn't ask for, the parts that were closed off when you were shaped into adulthood.

What Freud calls disposable libido lurks there. Those things that you were not allowed to do now suddenly become interesting. For example, you know the story about the man of middle age who has now learned to do everything he was taught to do and thought should be done. He does it all easily, so he now has spare time.

What does he do with his spare time? He suddenly thinks, "Oh, all those things that I deprived myself of in order to achieve all this!" Besides, the achievement itself becomes less and less interesting. I don't like to tell my college students this, but actually it's not worth it. You think, "Oh, those things I gave up!"

In any case, Daddy begins to see those little twinkle eyes over there that he hadn't been noticing before. The young girls somehow seem to him more marvelous than he remembers them to have been in his own youth, and the family begins to say, "What has happened to Daddy?"

Or he may have planned to earn everything and then retire. What was he going to do when he retired? He was going to devote himself to the love of his youth—let's say fishing. So he equips himself with a considerable amount of ritual gear, certain kinds of hats, rods ("You mustn't call it a pole; this is a rod"), silver doctors, and all kinds of flies that he's stuffed into his hat, and fine: the old man, he's got it all now. Let him have what he likes, let him go; he's got a hunting lodge and all that.

So what's he doing? He's fishing; that's what he was doing the last time he loved something, when he was twelve years old. What does he pull up? Fish. What is his unconscious waiting for? Mermaids.

He has a nervous breakdown—this is no joke; this is a phenomenon that the United States can document, millionfold: the man who thought he knew what he was working for. He was working to go fishing. Then he suddenly found that he was married, had kids, and had to work like hell, and everybody was sort of helping him get through this with the hope that someday he would retire and do the thing he wanted to do. Meanwhile, something inside him had grown up further than he had; he isn't ready for fish, he still wants girls, and that's not what's available. So he goes to a lunatic asylum, where these Loreleis come out of his own unconscious in very unappetizing shapes. That's the power of disposable libido.

Or Mother; we all know Mother: she's given her life to us, she's given everything she has to us. Perhaps she's also had some nice lovers and so on besides that sturdy old bastard that we call Daddy. Then the kids go away, so it's an empty house. So it's an empty life, and on comes this fury to grab life again. It's gone, it's gone, everything she'd given herself to, everything she's thrown her libido into is gone.

She goes crazy; she becomes what's known as a mother-in-law. She's bringing up your kid, she's telling you when to shut the window, when to open it, how to fry the eggs—all this kind of thing. This is a terrible crisis. These powers of the interior psyche come up in a compulsive way—the person can't help it—and you can sometimes see the person thinking, I mustn't do this. And then, by God, she's doing it again.

The old mythologies had to take care of this problem, too. They had to carry people from dependency through being the one who's carrying the universe to being somebody who isn't wanted anymore. Well, the old societies had a wonderful idea: old people are wise. So everybody made believe, you know, and the old folks were asked for advice and consent, and they'd give it. You had the council of the elders, the senate, and the society found a way to keep the old folks involved.

I've been connected for a few years now, in one way or another, with the State Department. Now, the people down there tell me that one of their great problems is *not* to do the things that the ambassadors and president and cabinet tell them to do. The State Department is a group of very learned individuals: they know what to do. However, they're only agents; the directions come from people who poured money into the Democratic or Republican Party for the election and so became ambassador to this, ambassador to that. These are the elders. And they're telling these professional diplomats what to do. I've heard from many of the State Department people that their main problem is to achieve the work as slowly as possible in order to bring about as little damage as they can.

The authorities are the old people. We haven't learned how to handle them today, but in the old traditional societies they had. The reason they'd learned was that nothing much changed from generation to generation.

Things passed in the times of the old people just about as they do in the present. So you could ask the elders how things used to be done, and the answer had some bearing on what should be done now. That's not true anymore.

There is one last transition for which a mythological order needs to prepare us: the journey out the dark door.

There's a little story I once heard about Barnum and Bailey's Circus. It used to have a special tent for the freak show. You paid fifty cents or so to go in and see the freaks, and you'd see all these signs: "To the Bearded Lady," "To the World's Tallest Man," "To the Living Skeleton," and all this sort of business. There were so many things to see that people were not going out, and the tent was filling up. This became a problem: what do you do with people who won't go out? Somebody had the wonderful idea to take down the exit sign and put up a sign that said, "To the Grand Egress." Of course, everybody went to see the Grand Egress.

We have a little story like that to help people die. You're going out the door, and it's going to be simply wonderful out there. There are going to be harps to play, everyone is going to meet you, and so on.

When the society begins to say, Now we really don't need you here, and we don't need you there either, the energies go back into the psyche again, and what are you going to do with them?

I was in Los Angeles recently, and I saw a lot of old people standing on the corner. I asked the person I was with, "What are they waiting for?"

He said, "They're waiting for the bus to Disneyland."

Well, that's one way to take care of people. All Disneyland really is, you see, is a projection outward of the phenomenology of the imagination. And if they can't go into their own imaginations, they might just as well go into Walt Disney's and he'll help them.

And that's what religions have done all this time. They provide something to think about in the way of divine beings and angels and how it's going to be out there. That gives you a lot of entertainment and keeps you from being too much of an annoyance to your daughter-in-law or whoever it happens to be who's got to worry about what to do with you. The TV's out of whack today.

Now, it's a basic mythological principle, I would say, that what is referred to in mythology as "the other world" is really (in psychological terms) "the inner world." And what is spoken of as "future" is "now."

I once overheard the clergyman at an Anglican wedding ceremony say to the couple something like this: "Live your life in such a way that you will merit eternal life in the future." I thought, Well, that's not quite correctly phrased. What he might have said, I thought, was this: "Live your life, your marriage, in such a way that you will experience your eternal life now." Because eternity is not a long time.

Eternity is not future or past. Eternity is a dimension of now. It is a dimension of the human spirit—which is eternal. Find that eternal dimension in yourself, and you will ride through time and throughout the whole length of your days. What helps to reflect the knowledge of this transpersonal, transhistorical dimension of your being and experience to you are these mythological archetypes, these eviternal symbols that live in all the mythologies of the world, that have been the support models of human life forever.

Myths for the Future

What can we see today? I think it's obvious from the bit I've talked about here that mythology has a function, that it takes care of this creature man, too early born. It carries us from infancy to maturity, from maturity to our second infancy, and then out the dark door. You know how most of the mythologies have told us Daddy and Mother will be out there, the old ancestors, Daddy God, Mother Goddess: you'll enjoy it, all your old friends, go on, don't be afraid to die. It's a sort of psychological nursery school.

There's an image that came to me long, long ago: the other animal that's born too early is the marsupial—the baby kangaroo or wallaby or opossum. These are not placentals; they can't stay in the mother's womb long enough to grow up. So, born at the gestational age of about eighteen days, they crawl up the mother's belly into a little pouch. There they attach themselves to a nipple and remain until they are able to get out and walk.

They are in a second womb, a womb with a view.

I think of mythology as the equivalent organ for man. We need mythology as the marsupial needs the pouch to develop beyond the stage of the incompetent infant to a stage where it can step out of the pouch and say, "Me, voilà: I'm it."

Now, in order to aid personal development, mythology does not have to be reasonable, it doesn't have to be rational, it doesn't have to be true; it has to be comfortable, like a pouch. Your emotions grow in there until you're safe to get out. And with the dismemberment of the pouch—which is something that has happened in our world—you don't have that second womb. The rational attitude has said, "Oh, these old myths, they're nonsense"; it has ripped the pouch to shreds.

So what do you have? You have a lot of missed births that didn't graduate from the second womb. They were thrown out, naked and squiggling around, too early and had to work it out for themselves.

How would it be if a little fetus were thrown out into the world? It's tough enough just to be an incubator baby, but without this marsupial pouch, without this mythological pedagogy, the psyche comes out all twisted.

Now, what has happened in our modern tradition is that science has disqualified the claims of our major religions. Every cosmological claim of the Bible is refuted; it's a ridiculous image of the universe in contrast with what you see when you peer through a telescope in the Mount Wilson Observatory. It's a ridiculous image of history when you look into the abyss of the past opened by archaeologists and paleontologists.

Our whole dependency on this concept that God is not in us but in this holy society has been completely wiped out. No one can honestly say he believes these things; he fakes it: "Well, it's okay, I like to be a Christian."

Well, I like to play tennis. But that's not the way we're taught to take it, and so we become disoriented. Add to that the coming in of Oriental, Congolese, Eskimo ideas. We are in a period that Nietzsche called the period of comparisons. There is no longer a cultural horizon within which everybody believes the same thing. In other words, each one of us is thrown out into the forest of adventure with no law; there is no truth that has been presented in such a way that you can accept it.

The whole point of science is that there are no facts, only theories. You don't *believe* these things; they are working hypotheses that the next bit of information may transform. We're taught not to hang on, but to stay open.

Can the psyche handle it?

There has been one other time in Western civilization when the culture's various myths were at odds in this way. During the last years of the

Roman Empire, the Near Eastern religion of Christianity had been imposed on the European individualism. Where the biblical tradition emphasized the need to subordinate the self to the holy society, the European tradition placed the greatest value on individual inspiration and achievement. During the twelfth century A.D., there was a terrific break between these warring traditions in Europe. It is best represented, if you have a literary bent, in the Arthurian romances, where these knights, parading as Christian heroes, are actually Celtic gods; gods of the Tristan romance, where Tristan and Iseult, like earlier Heloise, said, "My love is my truth, and I will burn in hell for it."

This conflict led, eventually, to the Renaissance and the Reformation and the Age of Reason and all the rest of it.

I think where we need to look now is to the same source that the people of the twelfth and thirteenth centuries did when their civilization was foundering: to the poets and artists. These people can look past the broken symbols of the present and begin to forge new working images, images that are transparent to transcendence. Not all poets and artists can do this, of course, because many poets and artists have no interest in mythic themes, and some who have an interest don't know much about them, and some who even know quite a bit about them mistake their own personal life for human life—the anger that's theirs is supposed to be everyman's. Yet there have been great artists among us who have read the contemporary scene in ways that allow the great elementary ideas to come shining through all the time, portraying and inspiring the individual journey.

Two of the great artists who have guided me in this manner are Thomas Mann and James Joyce. Just take *The Magic Mountain* and *Ulysses.* There you have the whole contemporary scene—at least as it was around the First World War—interpreted in mythological terms. Well, you'd be more likely to find equivalences to the experiences of Stephen Dedalus and Hans Castorp than you would to Saint Paul. Saint Paul did this, that, and the other thing, but that was far away in another land millennia ago. We're not riding horses these days, or wearing sandals—at least, most of us aren't. On the other hand, Stephen and Hans are in the modern culture field. They're having experiences relevant to the conflicts and problems that you're experiencing, and they are consequently models for you to recognize your own experience.

CHAPTER II

MYTH THROUGH TIME[17]

THE SURFACE AND SUBSTANCE OF MYTH[18]

One might reasonably define mythology as other people's religion. The definition of religion is equally uncomplicated: it is misunderstood mythology. The misunderstanding consists typically in interpreting mythological symbols as though they were references to historical facts. And this problem is particularly crucial in our tradition in the West, where the whole emphasis has been on the historicity of the events on which our churches are supposed to have been founded.

One finds the same basic mythological themes in all the religions of the world, from the most primitive to the most sophisticated, from the North American plains to European forests to Polynesian atolls. The imagery of myth is a language, a lingua franca that expresses something basic about our deepest humanity. It is variously inflected in its various provinces.

Adolf Bastian was a very great German medical man, traveler, and anthropologist back in the nineteenth century; in the 1860s, the University of Berlin created their chair of anthropology in his name. Bastian had traveled a great deal, paying considerable attention to the customs of the people he encountered. The universal and local aspects of the symbols he encountered stimulated him. To describe the universal aspect, he coined the term *Elementargedanke,* the elementary idea. Of course, there's no such thing as an elementary idea presenting itself to you raw; it always comes in terms of the way the particular culture is experiencing it. So he coined another term: *Völkergedanke,* or ethnic idea. The elementary idea shows itself always in relation to a specific culture context, and that's the ethnic context.

For instance, when you study the myths and folklore of northern and eastern Europe, you find the depths of the dark forest and, within them, the constant threat of the terrible wolves. Then, when you turn to Polynesia, it is the depths of the dark seas and the terrible sharks that represent the threat.

Now, the anthropologist or sociologist will tell you that you can't compare these two mythic motifs. Northern Europeans are influenced by the forest and wolves, and Polynesians are influenced by the ocean and sharks, and that's that. But anyone who has seen the same play produced in two different locales, as I have, knows the fallacy of that thinking. The young Chinese gentleman playing Hamlet in Hong Kong isn't the same as the young Jewish gentleman playing Hamlet on Broadway. Yet you wouldn't call the Hong Kong production a Chinese play any more than you would call the New York production a Jewish play. The essential plot and the relationship of characters remain the same.

That mystery of the dark depths that transcends the horizon of consciousness is represented, then, by the dark forests in Europe and by the ocean depths in Polynesia. The consuming danger within that mystery appears in different guises, too: the wolf and shark are expressions of the same primal fear.

You can, then, read across myths and see—to return to the theater metaphor—not whether the person playing Hamlet is Chinese or Jewish, but what role the actor is playing at the moment. There is a continuity of roles, a circumscribed spectrum of parts to be played. And when a part speaks to you—whether in the costume of a wolf or of a shark—you know what it is about, and you don't have to have any professor tell you whether it is time to be scared.

This fact leads one to conclude that the primary reference of these symbols—the Virgin Birth, for example—cannot possibly have been to historical events. The historical event, if such a one occurred, would have spiritual significance merely as a physical manifestation of a symbol that had its own significance before the particular historical event occurred.

In the Christian tradition, there is a very decisive problem in distinguishing between the senses of the terms "Jesus" and "Christ." "Jesus" refers to a historical character; "Christ" refers to an eternal principle, the Son of God: the second person of the blessed Trinity, which exists before and after all the ages and is, therefore, not historical. The sense of our tradition is that the historical character Jesus is or was the Incarnation on earth of that second person of the blessed Trinity.

Now, the main point that would distinguish our tradition in this respect from (let us say) Hinduism or Buddhism is that we would say that this Incarnation was *unique*. That has had a special force in our tradition. Yet the main point of the Christian religion is not, certainly, that the Incarnation was unique in the case of Jesus Christ, but rather that this miracle—the eternal principle of Christ's birth, life, and death—should have some effect on the individual human spirit. There is a wonderful line from the German mystic Angelus Silesius: "Of what use, Gabriel, your message to Marie / Unless you can now bring the same message to me?"[19] Likewise, the great mystic Meister Eckhart states, "It is of more worth to God that Christ should be born in the virgin soul than that Jesus should have been born in Bethlehem."[20]

This point is tremendously important. Many of the images—which in our religion are dogmatically affirmed as having had historical reality—are very difficult today to interpret in historical terms. For example, the Assumption of the Virgin or the ascension of Jesus to heaven both lead us to a problem: where is heaven? Somewhere up in the sky? Our contemporary cosmology does not permit us to entertain that thought very seriously. We have a collision between these articles of faith and the historical and physical sciences, which we have to admit are ruling our lives, giving us everything that we live by from day to day. This collision has destroyed people's belief in these symbolic forms; they are rejected as untrue.[21]

Now, since the primary truth is not the historical but the spiritual reference of these symbols, the fact that historical evidence refutes these myths on the level of objective reality should not relieve us of the symbols. These symbols stem from the psyche; they speak from and to the spirit. And they are in fact the vehicles of communication between the deeper depths of our spiritual life and this relatively thin layer of consciousness by which we govern our daylight existences.

And when those symbols—those vehicles of communication between our greater and lesser selves—are taken away, we are left without an intercom. This split leaves us schizoid; we live in a world up in the head, and the world down below is quite apart. We speak of schizophrenia when people, split in half like that, crack up: they plunge back into the night sea of the realities down there, which they had not been taught about. They're terrified—by demons.

Here is a basic theological formula: a deity is a personification of a spiritual power. And deities who are not recognized become demonic; they become dangerous. When you have not been in communication with them, when their messages have gone unheard or unheeded, and when they do, inevitably, break through, your conscious life is overthrown. There is, literally, hell to pay.

Myths derive from the visions of people who have searched their own most inward world. Out of the myths, cultural forms are founded. Consider, for example, the great mythic image on which the whole medieval civilization was founded: the myth, that is to say (and it is a myth, a great one, the appeal of which is mythological rather than historical), of the Fall and Redemption of man. The whole of the medieval civilization was constructed to carry the message and grace of that Redemption to the world. And then, when you question the historicity of the facts on which this myth rests (or which rest upon the myth), and when you reject the rituals through which the myth was actualized, you have the dissolution of the civilization. The medieval civilization actually collapsed under the weight of the rediscovered Greek and Roman ideas—the European spirit of individualism—that brought on the Renaissance. Thus, a new civilization emerges that tallies the findings of consciousness with the inner truths of the psyche, one inspired by the new dreams, visions, beliefs, and expectations of fulfillment. That is to say, a social structure evolves that correlates the changeless psychological needs of the individuals to the newly perceived cosmology.

For myths, like dreams, arise out of the imagination. Now, there are two orders of dream. There is the simple, personal dream where you get tangled up in your own twists and resistances to your life, the conflict between wish and prohibition, the stuff of Freudian analysis, and so forth, all of which I will discuss later. But then there is another level of dream, which we call vision, where one has gone past one's personal horizon and confronted the great universal problems, the problems that are also those rendered in the great myths. For example, when you face great calamity, what is it that supports you and carries you through? Do you have something that supports you and carries you through, or does that which you thought was going to support you fail? That is the test of the underlying myth by which you live.

Now, you will remember that, in a traditionally based mythological culture, a functioning mythology essentially serves four fundamental functions: the mystical, the cosmological, the sociological, and the psychological.

In our present world, the cosmological and the sociological functions have been taken away from us. Our image of the cosmos is totally different from the image expressed by the religious traditions in which we have been brought up.

Likewise, the social order today is totally different from what it was in the days when those laws of Moses and so forth were composed. Today, we think of morality as something that human beings can judge, not an immutable truth handed down from the mountain: change the circumstances and the moral order changes. In my lifetime, it has changed enormously. The social laws of yesterday are no longer the laws of today. As a person who taught at Sarah Lawrence College for thirty-eight years, I can't tell you what I've seen in the way of the transformation of the erotic morality of young women. Things are different, that's all. If you try to judge today's actions by what my students thought thirty years ago, it just won't work.

These practical and scientific and sociological processes are riding along, evolving on their own, whether you like it or not. The basic psychological problems of youth, maturity, age, and death—and the mystical problem of the universe—these, however, remain essentially unchanged. Consequently, it is largely from the psychological standpoint that one can reinterpret, reexperience, and reuse the great mythical traditions that science and the conditions of modern life have rendered useless, uncoupled as they are from their cosmological and sociological reference points.

The Birth of Myth: Primitive and Early Societies

I want very briefly to turn to the basic historical aspect of our subject. There are three great periods in the history of the human race.

The first, the primitive period, extends from the dawn of consciousness until the development of writing. In some parts of the world, nonliterate societies exist to this very day. There, people live very close to nature. Their horizon, in time and space, is very close. They have no records of earlier days, and their notion of time and the past, consequently, is short. They live, so to say, in very close proximity to the timeless time of the beginnings. Grandfather's day is already the mythological age.

The great middle period comes along about 3500 B.C., beginning in the Near East, in Mesopotamia. You suddenly find cities and, with them, the invention of writing, mathematics, the wheel, kingship, states. All that crystallizes around the middle of the fourth millennium B.C., and the whole formation was diffused from Mesopotamia to Egypt, where it arrives about 2850 B.C.; next to Crete and India, around 2500 B.C.; to China, around 1500 B.C; and to America with the Olmec people, around 1200 B.C.[22] This highly styled, globally diffused tradition is of a totally different order from that of the primitive, nonliterate world.

Finally, we find the third, modern period, beginning in Renaissance Europe. We have the development of scientific examination and experimentation and the empirical interpretation of nature. And, of course, we find the development of the power-driven machine, bringing the mechanization and industrialization that have built a totally new, totally unprecedented world culture.

Now, in the first, preliterate period, we come across two main attitudes. One is that of the hunting people in the great northern plains—up in Canada, in the United States, in Siberia, in northern Europe, and elsewhere.

There, life centers on the hunt, and the men bring the food to people. One observes, in this broad geographic field, that a basically male-oriented psychology and sociology operate. It makes a big difference to the tribe whether a particular man is a good hunter or not. And since hunting people are continually in collision with other hunting people, it makes a difference whether or not he is a sturdy fighter. You have in these societies a great stress on, and a flattering of, masculine prowess. There is, then, great attention paid in such societies to masculine prowess: the cultivation and flattering of courage, skill, and success.

The culture lives on death. Its members are continually killing animals, and not only killing them but wearing animal skins, living in animal-skin huts, and so forth. They are living in a world of blood. Primitive people do not view the human and the animal levels as greatly separated, in the way that we do. To kill an animal or to kill a man, there's not much difference. So the psyche has to protect itself against this continual killing, killing, killing. And the idea that becomes dominant and saves the situation is this: *there is no such thing as death.* That animal which you have killed will be back if you perform a certain rite. If you return the blood to the soil, the life is passed on, and the animal will come back. You can still find this principle in the kosher laws of the Hebrew tradition, where the blood must be poured full:[23] the Hebrews were originally a hunting and herding people. You'll also find this mythology among the Caribou Eskimos of central Canada. The animal is regarded as a willing victim who offers himself to the weapons of the hunter with the tacit understanding that a certain ritual will be performed that will enable his life to be returned and he to give his body again.

These societies had such respect for nature that they would not kill more animals than they could eat. If they were to do something so wasteful, they could be quite sure that the animals wouldn't come back the next year. So they killed only as many as they actually needed, and they thanked the animals, performing a ritual so there would be food again. You don't have people strip-mining the earth when they respect it in that way.

Then comes our Western tradition, where man is made to use the animals and use the earth and all that kind of thing with complete disregard. "And God said, Let us make man in our image, after our likeness: and let them have dominion over the fish of the sea, and over the fowl of the air, and over the cattle, and over all the earth, and over every creeping thing that creepeth upon the earth."[24] The earth is simply that which has not been conquered yet; it is something to be utilized. That's a ruthless attitude.

I think it is about time I told a little legend. There's a rather charming myth that illustrates the view of the hunting peoples. This myth comes from the Blackfoot tribes of Montana. They had a way (as you may know) of driving buffalo herds over a cliff—a buffalo fall—and then slaughtering the animals at the bottom of the cliff. Now, this particular tribe was unable to get the nearby buffalo herd to go over the edge, and so it looked as though winter were going to come and they would starve.

Well, one morning a young girl goes out to get the water for her family. She looks up and sees the buffalo herd, up there by the cliff, and she says, "Oh, if you'd only go over the edge, I'd marry one of you." And what do you know! To her great amazement, a great number did stampede over, tumbling and crashing onto the rocks below.

Now, that was a wonderful, gratifying kind of experience—until the last old boy comes up to her. He says, "Okay, girlie, off we go."

"Oh, no!" she says.

"Well," says the buffalo, "just look what's happened here! You said that you would marry one of us if we went over the edge, and we went. So, come on. It's your turn now."

So off he goes with her and what's left of the herd, up the cliff and out onto the plains.

Not long after, the family wakes up and looks around—where's little Minnehaha?[25] Well, you know how Indians are: they can tell anything from footprints, so of course Daddy sees that his daughter has run off with the buffalo. Well, he thinks, for heaven's sake.

So he gets his walking moccasins and his quiver of arrows, and he goes off in quest of his daughter, following the buffalo's tracks. Presently he comes to a buffalo wallow, a mudhole where the buffalo like to roll around and get the ticks off and cool off. He sits down to think a bit.

And while he's sitting there, he sees a magpie come flying down to pick around. Now, the magpie is very intelligent, a sort of shaman bird. So the man says to him, "Oh, beautiful bird, have you seen my daughter around here? She ran off with the buffalo."

"As a matter of fact," says the magpie, "there's a girl over there with the buffalo herd right now."

"Well," says the father, "please go tell her that her daddy's here."

So the bird flies over and he starts picking around: there she sits, while all the buffalo are asleep. The big boy, her husband, is right behind her. The magpie says, "Your daddy's over at the wallow."

"Oh," she says, "this is very dangerous. These buffalo will kill him. Tell him to be quiet and wait and I'll come."

Presently the buffalo wake up. The one behind her—the big fellow—takes a horn off, and he says, "Go get me some water."

So she goes over with the horn, and there's Daddy at the wallow. "Daddy, Daddy!"

"I don't want you hanging around with these buffalo friends," says the father.

But she draws back. "No, Daddy! This is very dangerous," she tells him. "We can't go running away now. You wait; they'll go back to sleep presently, and then I'll come."

So she goes back to her buffalo boy. He takes the horn and, sniffing at it, grunts, "Fe fi fo fum, I smell the blood of an Indian." He gives a snort and a roar, and all the buffalo get up and they paw the earth and raise their tails and do a buffalo dance. Then they go down to the wallow, and when they discover Daddy, they trample him to death—not only to death but to pieces, so that finally you can't find a morsel of Daddy.

The girl's crying and crying. She says, "Oh, my daddy, my daddy!"

The chief buffalo responds, "Yes, yes, you're crying because your daddy's been killed—one daddy. But think of us, with our wives and children and mothers and fathers gone over the cliff, all for you and your people."

"Yes," she says, "but he was my daddy, after all."

Now, Big Boy is a compassionate kind of buffalo, and he says, "Well, I'll give you one chance. If you can bring your daddy back to life again, I'll let the pair of you go."

So she turns to the magpie and asks, "Will you hunt around and see if you can find a piece of Daddy?" And the bird starts picking around in the mud and, sure enough, comes up with a bit of Daddy's backbone. The girl takes this bit of bone and puts it down on the ground, spreads her blanket over it, and starts singing a magical song. Presently, something appears under the blanket—not moving. She picks up the blanket and looks: Daddy's there, all right, but he's not alive yet. So she sings some more. Presently, the man stands up.

The buffalo are amazed, and they say, "Why don't you do this sort of thing for us, too, when you have killed us?"

So a covenant was arranged, a pact between the buffalo community—the animal community—and the human community. The buffalo taught the humans a buffalo dance, which became the basic ritual of the buffalo-killing culture of the American plains.

This is the Blackfoot version of a myth we find in various forms among all these hunting tribes. You have a moment when the woman of the tribe and the shaman creature of the animal species form a compact, a kind of marriage of the two worlds. Thereafter, the animals offer themselves as willing victims to the tribe, with the understanding that their blood will be returned to Mother Earth for rebirth. It's a basic myth of hunting peoples across the globe.

When we move, however, to the tropical world, we have a totally different situation, and a different paideumatic mythology to fit that situation. *Paideumatic* is a word used by Leo Frobenius, the great student of African primitive cultures, to describe the tendency of a culture to be shaped by its physical setting—its climate, soil, and geography.[26] There, the basic food is vegetable. Now, anybody can pick a banana, so there's no particular prestige in being a good banana picker.

At the same time, the female becomes the more important sex, mythologically. Being the mother, the woman becomes the symbolic counterpart, the personification of the powers of the earth. She gives birth as the earth does, she gives nourishment as the earth does. So woman's magic predominates in these cultures.

Furthermore, there is a terrible theme that comes in—terrible to our minds, at least. It explores a strange mystery that makes itself evident in the jungle law of vegetable life. When you walk through the rain forest, you see decaying vegetation everywhere, and from that rotting mass, green, new life springs. The obvious lesson emerges: out of death comes life. And the obvious corollary is, if you want to increase life, then you must increase death! It is out of this syllogism that a whole system of ritual murder developed in the tropical plant zone, a brutal system based on the notion that the killing—the sacrifice—will bring forth new life.

A culture's rites repeat the underlying myth of that culture. One could—as I have—define a ritual as the opportunity to participate directly in a myth. It is the enactment of a mythical situation, and, by participating in the rite, you participate in the myth. In the primitive tropical cultures, there are many relevant myths and many horrific rites representing such myths in literal reenactment, the idea being that the repetition will serve to refresh the force of the primal event.

The basic myth of the primitive planting people is that, in the beginning, there was a time when there was no passage of time, and the beings were neither male nor female, animal nor human. Suddenly, one of them was killed; his body was cut up, and the parts were planted. Out of the pieces, then, grew the food plants on which people live, so that when we eat, we are eating a divine gift, the gift of a divine body—whose flesh is meat indeed, and whose blood is drink indeed. You recognize this motif, I hope.

Furthermore, at that very moment, male and female became distinct from each other, and you have the beginning of begetting as well as killing. So life, birth, and death come into the world along with this new food that must sustain that life. So, then, the rites by which the force in life—the grace, if you will—of that mythological moment is renewed are always vivid and, in most cases, pretty grim.

Paul Wirz, a Swiss anthropologist, observed a rather horrendous ritual among the Marind-anim of western New Guinea that embodies that archetypal myth. After the seasons of the boys' initiation into manhood, there was a three-day period of general sexual license, after which the final ceremony took place. Around the dancing ground danced and chanted all the people of the community to the beat of these great slit-log drums, whose sound was understood to be the voices of the ancestors. A young girl comes out, dressed as one of those anonymous beings of that mythical age. She is made to lie down beneath a great lean-to made of prodigious logs supported by two uprights. Then the boys who have just been initiated—youngsters in their early teens—have their first sexual intercourse with this girl, in series, beneath that sloping ceiling of heavy logs. When the last of the boys is with her, in full embrace, the uprights are withdrawn, the lean-to drops on the couple, and they are killed. They are then drawn out, chopped to pieces, cooked, and eaten.

Represented here you have the reunion of the male and female; you have the reunion of begetting and killing. Here, too, is the idea that all eating is a eucharistic communion. This rite provides a tremendously vivid representation of the essence of life. Now you can see what I mean about rites that lead you to affirm life as it is. This ceremony is a reenactment of the mythological moment in the way of a conscious affirmation, not only of life but also of the horrific fact that life feeds on death.

Finally, in the pair being withdrawn from the rubble, cut up, cooked, and eaten in a communion meal, you see plainly the primary reference of all of the rituals of the slain and consumed deity. These youngsters represent the divine power.

Of course, when you have this women's mythology in the planting world, the men haven't a darn thing to do. In some of these cultures, they don't even realize that sexual intercourse has anything to do with birth. The women are building the houses. The women are raising the kids. The women are tilling the planting plot. So what have the men got to do? Well, there's a good condition for a masculine inferiority complex.

If nothing else, however, the males know how to compensate. They do what boys have always done and start a boys' club—the men's secret society, where no women are allowed. And within that society, you can have spiritual fulfillment and things to do.

Now, the model for this is the pattern in Melanesia. Think what the problem is: how to get away from Mother. No place to go. Women running the whole show. Not only are they running the whole show, but they're attractive creatures. That's the nasty thing about it. And you don't want to get away, you might say.

So here's the way they do it: by raising pigs. There are two stages to this: one for the little boy, and another for the big boy. The father gives the youngster a pig as a pet. And the boy is weaned away a little bit from his mother to the pig; he is the one responsible for this little creature. So he's learning not to be dependent but to be accountable. And as soon as he's become completely committed to this pig, Daddy helps him sacrifice the pig, so he's learning now to sacrifice what he loves. And then, after that has been fulfilled and he has swallowed this sacrifice, he's given another little pig.

After a little while, another phase comes into the masculine life, namely that of competition. The competitiveness, too, is transferred to the pig; this is done by knocking out the upper canine teeth so that the lower tusks can grow without interference. They grow out and around in a curve and come right back, curiously enough, through the jaws of the animal. Now the animal begins to suffer. So the animal is not putting on any meat. It's a thin, spiritual pig. You know how thin spiritual people can be.

In any case, the tusks grow right around in another circle, and you can, by great luck and very great care, get a three-circler. At each stage in the growth of the tusks, there is a sacrifice that the man has to perform of hundreds of other pigs that he has raised, so that by the time you get a three-ringer, that thing's worth innumerable other pigs. And with each sacrifice, the man's name can be changed; his spiritual rank changes, too, just as if he were a Mason.

We've had the simple, masculine Boy Scout mythology of the hunting world. We've seen the feminine mythology of the planting world. Now we have the masculine mythology of spiritual rank. And at each stage in this, he learned something more about the mystery of the underworld. The whole labyrinth motif is associated with this mythology. Think what's happening now. The man's spiritual life is linked to the length of his pig's tusks, which become emblematic of his growing inner stature. This pig is now a spiritual pig.

Before the man dies, he must sacrifice that great big porker, with all its rings; in so doing, he absorbs the power of that pig. Now, if he dies before he has sacrificed the pig, nobody else can dare to sacrifice it, unless he himself has a porker with at least the same number of rings, because his spiritual power would not survive the unbridled energy of that pig.

Finally, the man has died, and he is on his way now to the underworld with the spiritual power of that pig. And he meets the female guardian of the underworld, who, as he approaches, draws the labyrinth of the path of the underworld and then erases half of it. The man has to know how to draw it again, which he has learned through the secret society. And he presents the spirit of the pig that he has sacrificed for the spirit to eat, and he goes through to the realm of the dance in the flames in the volcano of the underworld.

Now, this may all seem pretty primitive and distant. But, you know how the Buddha died? This has been a little puzzle to a lot of people. He died from eating pork. A smith named Cunda invited the Buddha to a meal when the Buddha was eighty-two years old. And the Buddha goes with a little group of disciples to the meal, and the smith is serving luscious, juicy pork and a lot of vegetables. Well, the Buddha took one look at the meat and said, "Only one who has achieved *nirvāṇa* has the power to eat this pork. I will eat it. It is not to be served to my disciples, and that which is left over must be buried in the earth." That is a continuation of this theme of the pig.

Many of the great dying gods were killed by pigs or people associated with pigs. Osiris's brother Set was hunting a pig when he found Osiris and killed him. Adonis was slain by the boar. In Ireland, the Celtic hero Diarmid was slain by a boar, whom he slew simultaneously. In Polynesia, one of the principal deities is Kamapua'a, the youthful pig lord, who is the lover of the volcano goddess, Madame Pele. This is a mythology that stretches all the way from Ireland across the whole tropic world, and it is the first mythology that we have of spiritual rank and the surrogate death. In every one of these cultures, there's cannibalism—real or symbolic—and the highest power is to kill a man and absorb his energy. *Hic est corpus meum.*

These rituals—the buffalo dance on the one hand and the crushing of the mating couple and pig society on the other—represent two quite contrary worldviews. The deeper, the more tragic, is the view of the tropic world, where the image of life living on death dominates. The view of the hunters is, by comparison, a boyish, simple, careless view: nothing new is happening; we go back and forth repeating the same old things.

Now, since the first great high civilizations of the world emerged in hot, fertile southwest Asia, based on agriculture, they carried on that imagery of life out of death. We have the mythology, for example, of the Christian tradition: out of Jesus' death comes our eternal life. That's the whole background of the image of the Crucifixion. You find it even earlier than that in the imagery of the myths of Osiris, Attis, Adonis, and Dionysos.[27] The Eleusinian rites recapitulated this myth. Here is a continuity that constitutes an insight into something about life. It isn't an absolute truth about life, but it's an insight; it's a game that one can play. And the view of the world one has—if one goes through one's life playing the life-out-of-death game—differs totally from that of someone living the myth game of a hunter.

In any case, it is from the planting zone that the Neolithic emerges with the first permanent settlements. These are the beginnings of our higher civilizations, and these rites of sacrifice, which represent the myth in a very crude, outright physical form, become sublimated. Over the centuries, they become spiritual and symbolic, so that the food that is to be experienced is not simply physical food: it is food for the spirit. We have symbolism in our Buddhist, Hindu, and Christian rituals, sublimated out of a base that is common to all mankind.

Around the ninth millennium B.C., these societies take root and develop based on agriculture and animal husbandry. Suddenly, the tribe is cultivating food, not foraging for it.

Now, in the earlier, foraging societies, all of the adults were equivalent and of equal status: together they controlled the whole culture.

As I said earlier, the high cultures begin to emerge in what is known as the "nuclear" Near East beginning around 4000 B.C. Villages became towns, cities, and city-states. Trade and various new crafts and arts of civilization flourished; the individuals no longer controlled the whole communal heritage. They became "part" people, specialists. There are special governing people, priests, trading people, peasants, and so forth. And these people had to lead a life in harmony with people of a totally different kind. This hieratic structure brought about a whole new problem psychologically, sociologically, and every other way.

Most important at this tremendously important age are the priests. They are the ones who observe the heavens for omens to know when one should plant and when reaping time comes. It is the priests—particularly in Sumer—who first employ the arts of writing and mathematical observation. They are the ones who develop mathematics to describe the world: the sexagesimal mathematics of six, twelve, and sixty by which we measure time and space to this day.

These were also the first people to discover the movements of the planets through the fixed constellations; they recognized that the planets move in a mathematically predictable progression. These patterns of movement led them to conceive the idea of a cosmic order: a universal cycle writ large, so to speak, in heaven. The moon rises, comes to its full, and wanes. The sun daily rises and sinks. The winter leads to spring, to summer, and so forth. This idea of a great cycle, ever returning, struck the watchers of the heavens as a revelation, altogether more wonderful than the revelations either of the plant or animal kingdoms, superior to these, and to whose laws all things were bound. It was the revelation, namely, of a universal process, an impersonal, implacable power. You can't pray to the sun to stop—you can't pray to anything to stop. It's a process, absolutely impersonal and mathematically measurable, to which the ordinances of civilization should be brought into accord. That's the basic mythic concept of the first high civilizations.

THE BIRTH OF EAST AND WEST: THE HIGH CULTURES

With that foundation in mind, then, let us briefly review the whole range of the great high culture field. I divide the high cultures into two great domains: the Orient and the Occident. The line dividing these two domains passes right through Persia.

Eastward of Persia, in the Orient, there are two great creative centers: one is India and the other is the Far East, Japan, China, and Southeast Asia. Both zones are isolated. North of India rise the great Himalayas, and the borders give way to the oceans. East Asia is cut off to the west by the great deserts and to the south and east by the water.

Newly arriving influences can be absorbed gradually by the powers and traditions already there, so that, in the Oriental cultures, you cannot help but recognize the preservation—essentially to the present day—of the ancient, Bronze Age worldview which was brought in from Mesopotamia between 2500 and 1500 B.C.: the image of the great impersonal cycle.

Westward of Persia, there are also two great creative culture centers. One is the Near East or Levant, where the first high cultures emerged; the great stress there is on the society, on the group—not on the individual but on the participation of the individual in the collective. And the other great culture zone is Europe, which is the archetypal zone of the Paleolithic hunt, which, as in the primitive hunting cultures, stresses the individual.

These two areas—in contrast to the two Oriental zones, which are isolated—remain in continuous interplay. Furthermore, each zone lies open to attack by one of the two terrifically violent and ruthless warrior peoples who have been pushing in from north and south, respectively, on the settled farmers and traders of the middle area. These invading groups are the Aryans—from the cattle-grazing and herding plains of northern Europe—and the Semites—from the Syro-Arabian desert area, with their sheep- and goat-herding societies. Wherever they gained control, they became the governing caste in a world of civilized agriculturalists, artisans, and merchants, whose mythic lore and style of life were controlled by the findings of the priestly watchers of the skies. These two warrior groups honored a masculine divinity, a lord of thunderbolts. Their mythologies stand in diametric opposition to those of the land-based groups, who revere the goddess Earth, who sends forth her riches for her children. The principal divinity is the great goddess Mother Earth.

The conflict between the societies that have reverence for the goddess and these warrior people who despise them is one of the main motifs in the mythologics of the Occident. The Old Testament is the story of the conflict initiated by the warrior god who declares, "Those fields you did not plant you shall reap; houses you did not build you shall inhabit."[28] You can read it in the Book of Joshua: a simple little town, a dust cloud on the horizon, and the next day there's not a person living. Some Bedouin tribe has come in and annihilated them. The Greeks and Celts and Germans had the same idea. These were terrific fighters, these Aryans and Semites: fierce, tough people—barbarians. They came in and became the dominant people in cultures that had been designed around the idea of the continuously turning cosmic cycle.

In that mythology of the cosmic order, the whole sphere of the universe is the womb of the Mother Goddess, whose children we are. And the deities who make her fertile are usually represented in animal forms. These consorts are secondary to her. She is the primary divinity. The first object anybody experiences is Mother. Daddy is second. He can't put in claims. Who wants Abraham's bosom?

With the warrior people, however, you have a masculine god at the center: not one who prays to the goddess to bring forth the fruits of the earth, but one who comes in and takes them. He is the thunder hurler, whether his name is Zeus or Yahweh or Indra or Thor.

When you turn in particular to the Semitic people, who come from a desert, where Mother Earth doesn't seem to be doing very much for you and your life depends on the social order, the main deity of all the Semites, whether the Amorites or the Babylonians or the Hebrews or the Arabs or the Phoenicians, is the tribal deity. This is unique in history.

Now, if my principal deities are the nature deities, I can go from, let's say, Greece to India, and I can say, Oh, your Indra, he is our Zeus. You have that name for him, just as bread is bread whether it's called *brot* or *pain.* One deity is interchangeable with another, no matter what you call him. But when your principal deity is your tribal deity, you cannot say that your deity is my deity. So there's a tendency to exclusivism in the Semitic tradition, an excessive emphasis on the masculine figure, and out of this comes a sense of separateness: we are different from everybody else in the world.

The Greeks and Romans tended toward syncretism, to see in the other deities one's own. When you try to identify your particular myth, one question you might ask is what your relationship is to your deity, as opposed to the deities of other people, if you know who your deity is. What do you say? This is unique? There's nothing like it in the world? Or will you say, I participate in the life experience of other human beings, but I call it by this particular name? And this doesn't mean that you can't think yours the best way for you. But it's not right to go around saying, as there are people who do, Yes, you worship God in your way, I worship God in *his* way.

In any case, you now have a very interesting conflict between a patriarchal culture that is less refined but physically more powerful, and a goddess-worshipping civilization of much higher sophistication. Of course, the barbarians dominated, and then assimilated the local mythology.

Look at Genesis. Whoever heard of a man giving birth to a woman? Yet we find this silly thing in the Garden of Eden with Adam giving birth to Eve; the male is taking over the role of the female. In Hebrew, *adam* means "earth." So humankind was born from the earth; and yet, it is from an earthly father, not an earth mother.

Now, on Ash Wednesday you see lots of Catholics walking around the streets of New York with ashes on their foreheads. "Dust thou art, and unto dust shalt thou return."[29] Dust! That's Mother Earth, and you're putting her down that way? So you have this bachelor deity—this is the only mythology in the world without a goddess, the only one in the world. And the goddess of the other mythologies is called the Abomination.

The whole Old Testament has to do with the masculine Yahweh condemning the cult of the hills and the fields and the Mother Earth. One king after another does evil in the sight of Yahweh, building altars under the trees and on the mountaintops, one after another. And then some maniac like Elijah gets going, there are bloodbaths—whoever made eyes at the moon. It's really quite a story. So this is the horrific masculine mythology that we've inherited, which demands that we repress the female system.

One of the most interesting things about the Bible, which researchers turned up throughout the nineteenth century, is that all of the Old Testament mythological themes come right from the Sumero-Babylonian complex. Now, look what happens as a result. The myths that originally pointed to the goddess as the source of all now point to Yahweh, the male God. This transformation is a curious aspect of our tradition, even bewildering. Symbols talk spontaneously to the psyche; you know what they're saying, down in the unconscious. But the person who presents the myth to you talks a different language. He says, "It's the Father," but your psyche says, "No, it's Mother." So then we go to the psychiatrist. All of our symbols are speaking double-talk.

Thomas Aquinas states, in the *Summa contra gentiles,* "One can know God only when one knows that God far surpasses anything that can be said or thought about God."[30] When you then think of "that which surpasses all thought" as a male being—and, in our tradition, a male without a wife—you have something that the psyche just can't handle very well. I think this point is very important.

The stress on the sexual character of the deity—whether male or female—is secondary and, in certain contexts, baffling. It was originally oriented toward the masculine to establish the superiority of the patriarchal societies over the matriarchal. Both Aeschylus's *Agamemnon* cycle and Sophocles' *Oedipus* cycle attempt to resolve this problem, the male versus female systems.

Folks in the Orient don't have this problem. Eastward of Persia, in India and China, the old mythology carries the idea of the cosmic cycle—the impersonal order behind the universe—up into the contemporary world. You have the Indian idea of dharma and the kalpa, the Chinese concept of the Tao and so forth. These concepts, which are as ancient as the written word, transcend gender.

The notion is that the ultimate mystery of the universe, the ultimate being—if we can call it that—is beyond human thought, beyond all human knowledge. It is beyond even the categories of thought. It is pointless to ask, "Is it one or is it many, is it male or female, is it good or evil?" Those are categories of thought. It would even be meaningless to ask, "Is it or is it not?" Being and nonbeing are also categories of thought. It exists (or doesn't) absolutely beyond all thinking. It is transcendent of all categories.

It would be considered unsophisticated to ask, as we do, "Is the divine power loving, merciful, just—does it love these people more than those; does it love me?"

The next point, however, is that this power, which transcends all thought, is the very essence of your own being. It is *immanent*—it is right here, right now, here in the paper of this book, in the chair you're sitting in. You can take any object from this point of view and draw a ring around it and explore the mystery of its being, not knowing what it is because you can't know what it is. Fine, it's a chair, and you know what to do with it; however, its essential substance is ultimately and absolutely mysterious. The mystery of the existence of your chair is identical with the mystery of the existence of the universe itself. Any object, then—a stick, a stone, a human being, an animal—can be placed in the center of a mystery circle of that kind to serve as a perfectly proper source for meditation.

As early as the eighth century B.C., the Chāndogya Upaniṣad explicitly states the key idea: *tat tvam asi*—"You are it."[31] The whole sense of these religions—Hinduism, Jainism, Taoism, and Buddhism—is to evoke in the individual the experience of identity with the universal mystery, the mystery of being. You are it. Not the "you," however, that you cherish. Not the "you" that you distinguish from the other.[32]

The formula is a way of identifying yourself with the witness *and* with what is beheld. The commonsense view of the world is dualistic: I behold my body, I am not my body; I know my thoughts, I am not my thoughts; I experience my feelings, I am not my feelings. I am the experiencer, I am the witness. Then Buddha comes along and says there's no witness either. You can drive yourself out the back of the wall in this way.

And so we come to this point: anything that you can name is *not it.* That which you can name in yourself, you are not *it,* and yet you are *it;* that self-contradictory statement gives us the key to the mystery of what we call the Mystery of the East.

Yet it's the mystery of our own mystics as well. Many of them were burned for having called attention to these ideas. West of Persia, in the traditions that have come from the Near East—namely, Christianity, Judaism, and Islam—that is the prime heresy against the unbending truth: God has created the world; creator and creature are not the same.

Our theology normally lays things out from the point of view of waking consciousness: Aristotelian logic tells us that *A* is not *not-A*. But on another level—and it is this level to which all religions, even our own, finally refer, though they prefer to keep it buried—the ultimate mystery is that these two are one: *A is not-A*. Yet our official religions condemn as blasphemous anyone who says, "I and the Father are one." Jesus said it, and he was killed for that. That's what he was crucified for: blasphemy.

Nine hundred years later, the great Sufi mystic al-Hallaj said the same thing; he was crucified for it, too. And what did al-Hallaj say about this? He said this is what the mystic longs for: the orthodox community is there to unite the lover with his beloved, to unite the mystic with his god. He gave the image of the moth and the flame: the moth sees a light and comes banging against the glass and goes back to his friends in the morning and says, "Gee, I saw a wonderful thing last night." They say, "You don't look the better for it." Yet that's the condition of the ascetic. So he goes back the next night, and he finds a way in and he is united with his beloved; he becomes the flame. Said al-Hallaj, that's the aim of the mystic: complete extinction of ego sense in the knowledge of your extreme, ultimate identity with that one who is the One-of-All.

In our tradition, we do not emphasize the inner experience of identity with the divine. Rather, we emphasize the means of achieving a *relationship to* the divine. Ours are religions of relationship: *A* relates to *X*. Of course, in the Orient, *A equals X* and doesn't equal it, both at the same time. Relationship and identity are two different formulae.

So, how do you become related to the divine? In Judaism, you do it by being a Jew: nobody in the world knows God but the Jews—that was the old biblical idea. How do you become a Jew? By being born of a Jewish mother. That's pretty exclusive.

In the Christian tradition, Christ is seen as the unique Incarnation; he is true man and true God. We regard Christ's simultaneous humanity and divinity as a unique miracle. Well, how do you become related to Jesus? Through baptism and membership in a church.

So we are alienated from our divinity. Then we are alienated from the institution that claims to be in touch with the divinity because we don't believe it anymore. Christ rose from the dead, founded the Church, and so on? But what if he didn't rise from the dead? Was he really what he claimed to be? Born of a virgin, true God and true man and all that? Suppose you doubt that. Okay, the truth is taken away from you. The institution has taken divinity out of the world, put you in a relationship to it through an institution itself, and now the institution is gone, so you don't have any relationship to divinity at all. This is thoroughgoing alienation.

And then old Swami Satcitānanda comes along.

In the Orient, everyone is asked to realize their own dual nature; the incarnation—the avatar—is merely the model through which you find this miracle in yourself.

Now, I'm stressing this distinction because it shows the differing emphases in Occidental religions. They depend upon the historicity—the objective reality—of their special, favored situations. The Jewish tradition is based on the notion of a special revelation to a special people in a special time in a special place; this event must be historically documented. Well, as it turns out, the documents are questionable.

The Christian tradition depends on the idea of a unique Incarnation, on the evidence of miracles, and on the founding of the Church and the continuity in that Church. These events must all be presented as historical; that is why our symbols have been so consistently and persistently stressing the historical aspect.

Moslem belief relates the faithful to Allah through the word of Muhammad, his prophet.

That may be acceptable with respect to the institution of the Church or of Israel, or of Islam, but it distracts you from the symbol's primary reference: to you, inside. That's why the gurus come here from India, and the Zen masters from Japan: they're running off with all the chickens. They are saying that these symbols all point inside.

At the very opening of his wonderful book *Philosophies of India,* Heinrich Zimmer points out that our culture has come to a crisis that India faced some three thousand years ago: the total disintegration of the inherited myths. They can no longer be read in the concretizing way that is fashionable and almost inevitable in undeveloped societies. Now we realize, as the Indians then realized, that all of mythic force comes from within *us.* But it's got to come from within us. You can't take over someone else's inside, and we've got to go through the ordeal that India went through.

Now, I'm not saying that India's is a very much better case, because India has, since those days (900–400 B.C.), grown quite old. When you get old, things begin to fall out. Hair falls out, and you forget to change your clothes, and you've spilled and dripped things all over yourself. This is the way India looks. It is a disintegrated glory, and you mustn't confuse these two things. You can't, then, take over this decrepit old culture's way of handling its past and begin to bring it into yours. But you can listen, and you can let it inspire you.

And my little sermon to the churches of the world is this: you have got the symbols right there on the altar, and you have the lessons as well. Unfortunately, when you have a dogma telling you what kind of effect the symbol is supposed to have upon you, you're in trouble. It doesn't affect me that way, so am I a sinner?

The real, important function of the Church is to present the symbol, to perform the rite, to let you behold this divine message in such a way that you are capable of experiencing it. What the relationship of the Father and the Son and the Holy Ghost to each other might be, in technical terms, is not half as important as you, the celebrant, feeling the Virgin Birth within you, the birth of the mystic, mythic being that is your own spiritual life.

CHAPTER III

SOCIETY AND SYMBOL[33]

THE MECHANISM OF MYTHS: HOW SYMBOLS WORK

The way that mythologies work their magic is through symbols. The symbol works as an automatic button that releases energy and channels it. Since the mythic systems of the world include many symbols that are practically universal, the question comes up: Why? And how does the universal symbol come to be directed toward this, that, or another cultural intention? Now, this subject is rather intricate, but I think I can present it in a few clear lines.

Are symbols built into the psyche or imprinted afterward? Animal psychologists have noticed that if a hawk flies over little chicks that have just been hatched from the egg and have never seen a hawk before, they run for shelter. If a pigeon flies over, they do not. Models have been made of wood imitating the form of a hawk. When such models are drawn overhead on a wire, the chickens run for shelter; if the same model is drawn across backward, the chickens do not. Now, since we must have initials nowadays, this is called an IRM, or innate releasing mechanism, also known as a stereotyped reaction.

On the other hand, when a little duck hatches from its egg, the first moving creature it sees becomes, as it were, its parent. It attaches itself to this figure, and then this attachment cannot be erased. This on-birth bonding process is known as an imprint.

Now, the question with respect to the human psyche is whether the greater number of the responses are stereotyped or imprinted. The stereotyped response, as in the case of the hawk and the chickens, is a lock-key relationship, as though there were a precise image of that hawk etched into the brain of those chicks. You might ask yourself, Who is responding to the stimulus? Is it the little chicken, who has no experience of hawks? No. Rather, it is the chicken race, you might say.

The chicks' reaction to a real or constructed hawk exemplifies what Jung calls an archetype: a symbol releasing energy in terms of a collective image. Those chickens never experienced a hawk before, yet they responded to it. Whereas the funny little duck who has attached itself to a mother hen is quite peculiar in his way; he is an individual, not a mere type. The bond between duck and hen is the result of an imprint.

What distinguishes imprints from something you've simply seen and been interested in is that they come at a unique moment of psychological readiness, one that lasts for only a fraction of a minute. Once made, the imprint is definitive and cannot be erased.

As it turns out, we have found it impossible to determine any stereotyped images in the human psyche. For our discussion, then, we will have to assume that there are no stereotyped innate releasing images in the human psyche of very much significance. The imprint factor is the dominant one.

So then the question comes, Why is it that there are universal symbols? One can see in the mythologies, in the religions, in the sociological structures of every society the same symbols. If these aren't IRMs, built into the human psyche, how do these get there?

Since these symbols don't arise from inborn mechanisms and can't be culturally transmitted (cultures vary so widely), there must be some constant set of experiences that almost all individuals share.

As it turns out, these constant experiences are, in fact, in the period of infancy. They are the experiences of the child's relationship to (a) the mother, (b) the father, (c) the relationship of the parents, and finally (d) the problem of its own psychological transformations. These universal experiences give birth to the *Elementargedanken,* the unchanging motifs of the world's cultures.

SOCIETY, MYTH, AND PERSONAL DEVELOPMENT

Let me give a summary of Freud's thoughts on this matter so that we will have the basis for a discussion of the individual and society.

First, Freud based his model of psychology on the idea that there is a will, a desire, an "I want" that is inherent in the psyche. The psyche is a little "I want" machine, and the society or environment or the household itself or the incapacity of the child's body present prohibitions to the psyche's desires. Here we find the fundamental nuclear thesis.

The child cannot sustain the tension of wanting without resolution. In the face of the absolute prohibition—the thing that the child cannot, cannot, *cannot* have—the desire goes down into the unconscious. As Freud says, a good parent may distract the child from a forbidden or impossible desire by giving the kid something else to think about; that first "I want" stays there nevertheless, buried in the psyche as a wish.

The critical factor is that when the wish goes into the unconscious, the prohibition also goes. So, in the unconscious, there is a dynamic energy unit that contains both a positive and a negative; Freud calls this ambivalence. He calls this business of suppressing your wish and suppressing along with it a social prohibition introjection. One introjects a little chunk of the social order by that process. There is a built-in "no," a taboo, that is socially, not naturally, governed. This taboo differs from one society to another. Consequently, that which religious people call conscience is a social structure that functions as part of the moral system of the culture in which the child is born.

Let us take, as Freud does, the fundamental nursery association: the desire of the child for Mother and the mother's inability to satisfy the child all the time. This ambivalence—the wish and the prohibition buried together—lies in the psyche as an energy unit. Now, an energy unit in the psyche must be expelled eventually; there have to be moments of discharge. This discharge takes place on the unconscious level. That is to say, instead of wishing (as the child does) for Mother, the psyche finds a substitute wish. What you consciously think to be a perfectly moral activity—marriage, for example—in the unconscious services a completely immoral function:

incest. Under the table, so to say, you are enjoying an experience that is forbidden by the society, and you are forbidding yourself even to know that you are enjoying it.

This process forms the basis for the Freudian idea of neurosis. When an individual is full of anxieties and fears in a situation that is not fearful, these are not real anxieties. They are imagined punishments from invisible parental disciplinarians for prohibited desires that the individual has secretly enjoyed.

Now, when there have been an excessive number of frustrations, of prohibited desires, there is an irresistible down-pull in the psyche; that is to say, there is too much going on down below, and the individual may become incapable of action up in the conscious world. If the unconscious content piles up tremendously, you can have what is called a psychosis: the individual loses contact with the outside world altogether.

For example, when the suppressed childhood desires become adult desires and channel into genital sexuality, the notion of the mother as the object becomes a notion of incest, which is absolutely taboo—the adult does not even know that's the wish. Now, the incest wish is blocked both by the unconscious prohibition and the threat of punishment; this threat comes from the father image. Freud says the father is the first enemy; this is Father's role, and Mother manages to make it work by saying, "You wait till Father comes home." The mother transfers what is called bad-mother content onto Daddy, and he has this role.

Then Daddy has to serve as educator, inducting the child into a relationship with his adult world. Unfortunately, the child already has this curious ambivalence with respect to the father. The father, on the other hand, resents the child because the child has removed him from Mother—for a certain period, at any rate. So there's this mutual antipathy. Freud calls this opposition the Oedipus complex. By mistake, Oedipus killed his father and married his mother, which, Freud tells us, is what all little boys would like to do anyhow.

There is, of course, a reaction against the Oedipus complex; Freud calls this the Hamlet posture. Like Hamlet, the young chap says, "Oh, no, I do not want to kill Father. I honor my father greatly, and Mother, she is a terrible, terrible thing. She's tempting me all the time, and provoking me to kill my father." Just think of Hamlet's mess: he goes in and nearly destroys his mother. Then, of course, all that Mother represents—women, the world, the universe, life, being itself—becomes repulsive. You have these pure, pure souls who won't touch women but are bowing, bowing, bowing to the father image. This is a great overplaying of the reaction against being Oedipus, and it means that you really are, way down, just that. For Freud, all men are either Hamlet or Oedipus—or both.

The woman's problem is exactly the reverse: she suffers the fate of Electra, who finds that Mother is her rival for Daddy's love. Actually, according to this view, a girl's crisis comes at the age of about four, when the gender difference hits. She becomes aware of some of the implications of this divide. The girl has to shift her main attachment from the mother, which boys and girls share to this point, to the father. Father then becomes the educator of the daughter, giving her a relationship to the male. He has to play that role a little bit, giving the girl a sense of the male that differs from that of the horrendous opposite. This lesson takes place just as the father is inducting the boy into the realm of the social order. So the father actually plays the educator to the spirit, he transmits the goals of the society, he informs the child of the adult role he or she is expected to assume. The mother gives birth to the physical body; the father, to the spiritual being. These are motifs that occur over and over and over again in myths from the most sophisticated cultures and the most primitive.

Education on this primary level will ideally carry the psyche beyond that threshold so that adult challenges will produce an assumption of responsibility rather than a flight to dependency. The challenges to come will cease to bring echoes of the child's relationship to parent; they will bring instead an adult's relationship to some action that must be undertaken. This is the transformation that has to take place at the point of crisis and is a constant problem in all societies.

This crisis comes at the end of a period of dependency that lasts at least twelve years. During this time, we are incapable of caring for ourselves. What distinguishes the human species from all other kinds of animals is that we are born too soon. Actually, neither the human physique nor the human psyche matures until the early twenties.

Then comes the first crisis. This dependent little creature is expected to become one who doesn't turn for help to Daddy or Mommy but *is* Daddy or Mommy.

It is as though plaster of Paris had been poured into a mold of dependency, has begun to set, and then the plaster is suddenly asked to take the form of personal responsibility. The young adult psyche is supposed to move out of the dependent pattern into the adult pattern of responsibility—responsibility as defined, of course, in terms of the requirements of the specific society.

This phase of experience—from birth through the onset of adolescent crisis—progresses through more or less the same challenges that all human beings face. The growing up of the little psyche is timed in about the same way everywhere; then the individual must make that jump. And in every society, this transformation is a matter of deep concern. The initiation rites in primitive societies are concerned with precisely that moment. The individual is dealt with in such a way that he can no longer fly back to Mother. The educational ritual translates the inevitable, universal images of infancy into images that will link the individual to the society. The totem ancestor, the Mother Goddess, and all of those involved pantheons—the Vedic and Olympian and Navaho and Norse and Shinto gods—represent these early imprint images intentionally shaped so that the energies flowing to them are channeled into social attitudes that have significance in the world of the culture.

The main thing the society—any society—requires from you is that you be capable of assuming responsibility at the drop of a hat, without correcting yourself. The person who is torn between attitudes of dependency and responsibility is neurotic; he is ambivalent, he is pulled in two directions. Until he can face a challenge without running back to his parents internally, he can never be a true adult.

Eventually, the individual must face a return to dependence, the problem of losing that responsibility, that capacity which was a matter of such pride, and prepare to move through the dark gate. In order to prevent a pathological breakdown at this point, the mythology's images now have to induce the psyche willingly through that gate. Mother and Father reappear in a new way. The images that have served to bring the youth to the frightening activity of full responsibility now must be used to bring the declining years to the frightening inactivity of death. And, as we will see, this transition is the problem that most interested Jung.

THE EGO: EAST AND WEST

I want to bring in some terms that will be very important in my contrast between what appears, from my view of these matters, to be essential to European, Occidental thinking about the self in the society, and what appears to be essential to the thinking of the whole Oriental world.

Today, we have the idea of a two-story psyche, so to say. Down below lies the unconscious, while the conscious individual is above. This individual has a sort of flashlight in his hand: consciousness. Now, if I ask you what were you doing at 10:30 P.M. on such and such a day, you might not be able to recall for the moment. However, if you look in your date book and see "Party with So-and-so," it comes back very vividly. Here is something that's not in your consciousness now but is available; Freud calls that the preconscious.

If, however, I asked you what toy you played with on the third day of your life, you would not be able to find that out. That memory is way down in the unconsciousness, in what Freud calls the subconscious, the realm of thoughts and memories that are totally unavailable to the conscious mind. The important thing is that all of the primary imprints from the first four years of your life are down there, and by that time your little mind is all set.

Now, down in the subconscious is an "I want" machine that Freud calls the id. The id is what you're born with. When you're just born, the id within you doesn't know the date. It doesn't know whether it is the period of the ordination caves in the early Neolithic or the height of the modern age; it doesn't know whether you're born in Timbuktu or Washington, D.C. All it knows is that you are a human animal and that you have human needs. In other words, it is sheer organism, wanting something.

The environment says, "Don't, don't, don't." This interplay is the wish-prohibition conflict we talked about earlier. So you begin to take a lot of "I mustn'ts" down into the unconscious; the society's "I mustn't" counters the id's "I want." What Freud calls the superego provides the stream of "I mustn'ts." The superego is the internalization of the parental, societal voice, balancing out the id by saying, "Don't do this, do that."

According to Freud, ego is the function that relates the individual to reality. Reality in this terminology is nothing metaphysical whatsoever. It is empirical reality: what is here around you now, what you are doing, what your size is, what your age is, what people say to you and about you. Ego is a function that relates you to reality in terms of your personal judgment—not the judgments that you have been *taught* to make but the judgments that you *do* make.

You can judge a situation in terms of how you know you *ought* to judge it, and then you realize, I don't think of it that way at all. You may consistently differ from the judgment system that your environment has given you. Only if you have made the transition to adult responsibility are you able to make your own judgments and let society's judgments drop. Of course, if you are not really detached, they're not going to drop; they will keep drumming back at you with feelings of guilt.

Traditional cultures in the West differ here from those in the Orient. Oriental religious instruction tells one to cancel ego. In this tradition, one is told to behave in terms of the societal ideal dictated by the superego. There is no systematic development of the ego in relationship to reality or the individual situation.

Often, in conversation with someone from the Orient, if you ask a question having to do with *now,* the response is a deluge of all of the clichéd answers you can imagine. It is very, very difficult to get a reality judgment in terms of the immediate situation. Since the ego is not developed in the Oriental traditions, you don't get the same kind of response that we would expect in the West, with the individual taking responsibility for his own judgment, his own discernment.

When you turn to the Oriental systems and read the law books—the *Mānava-Dharmaśāstra* of India, for example—you can't believe what's done to people who don't follow the rules. In Sun-tzu's book *The Art of War,* he declares that for small faults there should be great penalties; then there will be no great faults.

The fact is that in Oriental religious vocabulary, ego is identified with id. So the individual system becomes "I want" versus "thou shalt." All ego is, according to this way of thinking, "I want." So the message is, cancel ego. We can find a similar message in traditional biblical teachings, which are full of "thou shalt, thou shalt, thou shalt." Both Oriental and orthodox Judeo-Christian instructions demand absolute obedience. What about a situation where your judgment says that something entirely aside from the "thou shalt" is required? How do you feel when you do the thing you're not supposed to do? This is one of our great problems.

As we have seen, the structure of Oriental society was laid down in the hieratic city-states of the Bronze Age, in and around Mesopotamia. The fundamental idea was that the heavenly order should be the model for the order of life here on earth. The macrocosm, the great cosmos, is an ordered cosmos. The society—the mesocosm, as it were—aspires to reflect that celestial design, as does the life of the individual, the microcosm. This is the Great Harmony.

We have also seen that religious imagery serves certain functions in mythic systems: to present the sense of awe and mystery before the fact of the universe of being; to give an image of the universe itself, which is that of the mathematical order of the cosmos, the sun and moon in their cycles, the year and its cycles, the eon and its cycles; to relate the society to those cycles; and to relate the individual to society, that cosmos, and that mystery. These are the functions of the mythology, and, if they are successful, you get a sense of everything—yourself, your society, the universe, and the mystery beyond—as one great unit.

Now, the individual in this system must fill a role within the order as dictated by the knowers of the order, the priestly group. They understand the order and decipher its pattern, while the individual participates as the priests dictate. This pattern is called, in Sanskrit, dharma. It is the order of the universe; the word *dharma* comes from the root *dhr,* which means "support." The support of the universe is this order. As the sun should not wish to be the moon, as a mouse should not wish to be a lion, so the individual born into one caste, one category of society, should not wish to be anything else. The individual's birth determines his role, his character, his duty, and everything else. In such a society, education consists of being trained to one's proper role.

In other words, what Freud would call the superego, the societal ego ideal, is to be the *sole* ideal. And the instruction is so severe on this point that individuals are never asked, "What would you like?" They are told; they are commanded from beginning to end, even in those most intimate moments of life, moments that are for Occidental people moments of personal choice, personal decision, personal discovery. These passages are dictated: one doesn't even know whom one is to marry; others decide for one.

There isn't that test of the growth of individual judgment in deciding what potential spouse one prefers; the society decides for you. The ego is completely erased.

One could summarize the basic religious view of the East somewhat as follows. The ultimate truth, the ultimate mystery of life and being, is absolutely transcendent. One cannot define the absolute. One cannot picture it. One cannot name it. Nevertheless, that which is absolute being and absolute mystery is also one's own inner reality: one is that. The absolute is both transcendent and immanent; that is to say, both beyond the universe of the senses and within each particle of that universe. All that can be said about it is... nothing. All that can be said *points* to it. Therefore, the symbols, the rites, the rituals, and the acts are involved in a world of human experience but point past themselves to that transcendent, immanent force; the rites and symbols lead one to the realization of one's identity with that absolute. Identity with the transcendent is one's essence; consequently, in Eastern philosophy, the mere accident of the ego, of the personality, is quite secondary.

Over in the Occident, there is a totally different idea. It came in around 2500 B.C., with the Semitic empires of Sargon and Hammurabi. The idea, which we still adhere to, is that God makes man. God is not man, and man is not of the same substance as God: they are ontologically, fundamentally different.

Consequently, all of the symbols have to do with *relationship*. You don't get that in the Oriental system. There, the gods—just like man—are simply manifestations of the greater order. That order is there, preexisting the gods themselves. In India, this order is called dharma; in China, it is called the Tao. In early Greece, it was called *moira;* in early Mesopotamia, it was called *me.* This cosmic order is mathematical and unalterable; not even a deity can initiate change. God and man are simply functionaries of that order. To become a responsible citizen, you must learn your job perfectly.

Well, let me give now as an illustration of the very formal attitude, the classical Indian social structure. I'd like to look at the classic notion of the individual life and its development.

Of course, there are four castes or classes. In India, the four castes are the *brahmin,* the *kṣatriya,* the *vaiśya,* and the *śūdra.*

Brahmin means "related to or in touch with *brahman,*" the cosmic power. *Brahman* is a genderless noun for the power that infuses and suffuses the whole world. The *brahmin* is the one who knows that and tells the truth about it and interprets and writes the holy books. The *brahmin* is the head of the social order.

The *kṣatriya* is the one who administers the true law. He administers what the *brahmin* tells him to administer; this is the ideal, at any rate. The *kṣatriya* is the sword-bearing arm of the order.

The *vaiśya* is the citizen or merchant. The word comes from the root *viś*, which means "neighbor." He is the man of money, the property owner, the landowner, the employer, and so forth. He pays his taxes, he pays his tithes, and he employs the *śūdras*. He's the body of the society, the guts.

The *śūdra* is the servant, who is excluded from the religious order. He has his own religious teachers and village priests and so forth, but the Vedic and traditional Hindu Brahminical order concerns the upper three castes only; these upper three castes are called the twice born. The *śūdra* is the legs of the outfit, carrying the rest of the society along.

Now the goal, as I've said, of the Oriental society is always to cancel ego, that ego should be wiped out. The *śūdra* cancels ego by doing what he is told. The *vaiśya* cancels ego by serving, by doing as he is told, by paying his debts and bringing his family up; his goal is to make money. The *kṣatriya* serves by administering the law with justice, without prejudice, and without favoring himself. He's supposed to represent the perfect administration of the law. The *brahmin* is to know the law.

This system has excluded the majority of the people, who are called the outcasts. In a census recently made of a Bengali village community, it was found that more than half of the people were outcasts; they are simply out. The only way they come in is in extremely menial and untouchable social functions. Otherwise, they have villages of their own, living, as it were, lives outside of the domain of the holy order.

The *śūdras* are the craftsmen and the peasants and so forth who function within the society. Of the remaining half of that village, 50 percent were *śūdras,* so that the group served by the outcasts was actually this peasant class. And you realize the fierceness of these divisions when you read one of the texts in the *Mānava-Dharmaśāstra,* the "Laws of Manu." It says if a *śūdra* hears a recitation of a verse of the Vedas—even by accident—he shall have boiling lead poured into his ears. I find it fascinating that he should be killed in that manner. The Vedic knowledge was power knowledge, and it had a social as well as a spiritual power to enforce.

As a result, when one is teaching or lecturing Oriental students even today, the experience is absolutely incredible for an Occidental: the students take it all in. The Indian idea, for example, of the guru is of one whose authority is absolute; the *śisa*—the student—simply receives it unquestioningly. The principal virtue of a student is in Sanskrit called *śrāddha*—namely, absolute faith in the teacher.

The guru accepts responsibility for your life. You try to live the life as the guru says it should be lived, and, in doing that, you're living his life, whereas the Western teacher simply dispenses information and you can fool around with it as you wish in terms of your own experience. I'm not telling you—and no Western teacher will tell you—what you must do when you're here on the path. There is no path. Particularly now, we are in a sort of free fall into the future.

We expect the student to develop a critical faculty. Now, some of your teachers may have felt annoyed by the criticism that came from you with your independent judgments—darn you. Yet if they were to deal with one of these situations where everything is taken in, trust me, it becomes hard not to say, "Holy God, I'm, *I'm*, *I'm* the law and the prophets and everything else." That doesn't serve education very well either.

Let me tell you a little Indian anecdote about a guru. A student arrives late one day to his guru, and the guru says, "Well, you're late; where have you been?"

The student responds, "I live on the other side of the river. The river is in flood. I couldn't ford at the usual fording place. There's no bridge and there's no boat—I couldn't get here."

"Well," says the guru. "You're here now. How did you get here? Did a boat come?"

"No."

"Did the flood go down?"

"No," replies the student. "I simply thought, 'My guru is my divine revelation; he is my god. I'll simply meditate on my guru, and I'll walk across the water.' So I said, 'Guru, guru, guru,' and I'm here."

Well, thought the guru, I didn't know this about myself. This bugged him, and he couldn't get it out of his mind.

When the student had finally gone, he thought, "I've got to try this." So he goes down to the riverside, looks to make sure that nobody is observing this experiment, and says, "I, I, I."

He steps out onto the flood—and sinks like a stone.

The only reason he was a guru was that he (so to say) wasn't there. He was transparent to transcendence until he had the thought *I*. The guru is supposed to be an absolutely perfect pane of glass through which the light of what he has been taught shines. So this wisdom that comes through the guru comes from the ages; it has nothing to do with this moment here and now, nor with the person who is transmitting it.

Dharma defines not only who you are but how you should lead each phase of your life. The first part of life is lived in the village. In the middle of this life, one leaves the world, and thus begins the second part of life, in the forest. By this wonderful device the Indians were able to combine something that we're not able to combine in our society. They were able to combine the idea of social duty—dharma—and the idea of escape, leaving it all: what is called *mokṣa,* or release.

This system is divided again in two: the first half of your first half of life is devoted to being a student, to learning the ways of dharma.

Now, the ideal for the student in India is *śrāddha,* absolute faith with perfect submission to the master. Through this perfect submission, the student is to concentrate all of his libido, all of his erotic interest, into the master. He is to identify with him to the very tip of his fingers. He is to imitate the master, to be like him, to become him. You have, you might say, a passing on of the image without any development of the critical faculty.

Next, at the passage to adulthood, the individual moves into the second part of the first half of life. The student suddenly becomes a householder. He dresses differently, and he has a whole new set of duties. He's married suddenly to a little girl he never saw before; she never saw him, they're not supposed to have known each other. Perhaps you can imagine the great crisis. It comes when the wall or screen is removed and each sees the other. And for the girl, this moment is particularly shocking because this man is her god, literally; she is to worship him.

They do their duty. So, before they're very old, they have a little family round about.

By the time the man is in his mid-forties, there's a son old enough to take over the household. The father has fulfilled his responsibilities; now he goes into the forest.

The whole village life has been devoted to doing what you're supposed to do, but a tincture of ego nevertheless remains. The individual now commits himself to the discipline of getting rid of ego entirely. In the forest, he finds a teacher; he becomes a *vānaprastha*—the one standing in the forest. Yoga— this is the real, severe yoga now—aims to eliminate whatever remains of ego.

When ego dissipates entirely, one enters the second half of the second half of life. One becomes a *bhikṣu,* a wandering monk, an oracle of the knowledge of nonbeing, of nonentity, of being without an ego.

Indians speak of the four things for which men live; this is a basic theme of Indian philosophy. Three of the things for which men live are in the village: one is virtue, or dharma; another is success, or *artha;* a third is pleasure, or *kāma.* Those are the things for which men live in the world.

When one goes into the forest, one seeks *mokṣa,* or release. Now, this word is often freely translated as "freedom." That is not what it means. It means release from ego itself.

Dharma is imposed by the society; the society tells you what your dharma is. The notion is that since you have come in, say, as a *vaiśya,* your soul has reached the *vaiśya* level; therefore, the ritual and laws of *vaiśya* life are proper for you. That is to say, the laws of society correspond precisely to your own personal needs, your readiness.

One style of yoga, *kuṇḍalinī,* gloriously develops the idea of the inter-play between *kāma,* the pleasure principle, and *artha,* the power principle. I find this tremendously interesting. These two drives—*kāma* and *artha*— correspond exactly to two components of our old friend the id: *eros,* the will to experience pleasure, and *thanatos,* the will to drive yourself through and experience power and success.

Now the Indian idea is that *artha* and *kāma* are nature's ends, while dharma is society's end. The function of the individual is to achieve his success and his pleasure under the ceiling of dharma. Then the ultimate spiritual experience comes in the forest, where you cancel ego according to disciplines announced to you by your guru. Now, that is the system that I would like to hold in contrast to the one that seems to me to be normal in the West: our tradition of ego development.

It fascinates me that, quite independently from the Indian system, Occidental psychology brings out this same notion of the power and pleasure principles. Yet where traditional Indian thought balances these two directly against societal virtue, or dharma, Freud interjects a mediator, the ego, which reconciles the inner desires of the id and the outer demands of the superego.

Now, there's just one more point. Freud divides the periods of early life into three stages. One is the stage of infancy, during which the child has all of the primary shocks. This stage lasts from about year four to year seven in a child's development.

Next comes what Freud calls the period of latency. This is the period of ego discovery, which lasts from about year seven or year eight to year eleven or so.

Finally, we get the movement into puberty and the development of genital sexuality. Throughout this period, the child moves away from what might be called infantile mythology—the commitments to the parents, the notions that the moon is following him when he walks, the idea that animals have communications with him and all that sort of spontaneous child imagery. It's during this period—what we call the teenage years—that the individual is encouraged to empirical reality and, in our culture, science. It's during this period that the child becomes gradually aware of a scientific, as opposed to mythological, attitude.

Primitive societies insist on the mythological attitude, as do Oriental societies. These cultures encourage the child to interpret the world in terms of the mythological patterns. Those years of adolescence are the critical years, and they're the years that in traditional Oriental societies do *not* produce the little scientific mind, the mind ready for critical judgments of reality and decisions of action and so forth on every single level.

In the West, we celebrate the scientific mind. But the symbols of our inherited traditions lie broken around our feet. Now there's a rather important point about religious traditions. Do the rites work without you having any connection to the myth, or do they not? This comes up in the matter of baptism, for instance. I remember in my youth a certain thug, a murderer, received baptism just before death. Now, that is supposed to clean you completely for immediate entrance into heaven.

I don't mean to judge the soul of this man, but I do mean to judge the tradition that says that, no matter what this man had done, once the water was poured over him and the proper formula spoken, something happened to him that we don't understand which made him eligible for entry in paradise. This is, I think, a crucial problem in the religious consciousness of man today; how many people can go with that? Normally the symbols of a devout religious tradition have to be taught to you; you have to know what they are meant to be saying.

But there are certain aspects of those symbols that, if they have not been too elaborately developed in the theology, actually work. I think the symbol of the crucified hero-figure works. This is a motif that occurs in many, many religious traditions. We find it among the Pawnee Indians, we find it among the Aztecs, we find it among the Mayans, we find it in the Prometheus figure, chained to the rock: the figure of the hero who, out of love, has brought the boon—the boon of atonement or the boon of fire or whatever it is—and for this purpose has given his own life, thoughtless of his own self.

This story hits home. You just have to be clued in a little bit for this; you don't have to worry about the relationship of the Son to the Father and to the Holy Ghost; all of those things are quite secondary to the power of the myth. The business of being made to feel the gratitude to the being who has either voluntarily or involuntarily given up its own life to be your life, your food and drink, spiritual or physical—this is a motif that has great significance. The call of a hero on the battlefield, giving his life for his country—this is a hero act equivalent to the Crucifixion. And I think images like this can still activate within you that aspect of your own consciousness and potentialities, which is the noble, the heroic, and the great.

CHAPTER IV

MYTH AND THE SELF

JUNG AND THE POLARITIES OF PERSONALITY[34]

I've mentioned C. G. Jung in passing, but it's time to look at his ideas more closely. You often hear from Freudian circles that Jung was Freud's disciple. This claim is absolutely false. They were colleagues, each with a particular focus on the processes of the subconscious mind.

In general terms, Freud saw sex as the main determinant in psychology. Children's relationships to their parents, as typically played out in the erotic relationship to the mother, the fear of the father, and then the transfer of the child's sexual commitments to an individual of his own age and so on—Freud saw the acting out of these sexual dramas as central to all human behavior.

Among psychologists, the first challenge to Freud's theory came not from Jung but from Alfred Adler. Adler said that the main drive in the individual is not sex but the will to power. Imagine: the little infant is in a great disadvantage with respect to its parents. It's there with these two giants, yet it must put through its purposes; it has to learn to wheedle or to frighten or one way or another to get the parents to do its will.

All infants initially hold inferior positions, but imagine that that child

63

grows to find itself truly inferior, unusually inept. Or suppose it has what Adler calls "some inferiority of the organs." Perhaps it belongs to a physical or behavioral type that is unusual in the neighborhood and is, therefore, for better or worse, outstanding and at the center of attention. Or suppose the parents have been brutal and the child hasn't been able to put its agenda through at all. It now has a will to compensate, to overcompensate, which leads to what Adler calls an inferiority complex. Adler feels that the drive to overcome a sense of inadequacy is fundamental to human life, that all individuals act from this impulse, not the sex drive. Indeed, Adler believes that sex is itself a field for the enhancement of one's own sense of value—a field for conquest. In other words, he interprets sexual activity itself as a function of the power drive.

At this point, Jung comes into the picture. Jung says that the psyche actually has a fundamental energy that manifests itself in each of these two directions—sex and power. He calls the tendency toward one or the other direction the basic attitudes.

In some people—possibly due to infant relationships—the stress manifests in a struggle for individual power, in which case the sexual life takes a secondary position. This type of person, oriented primarily toward power, is always asking, "How am I doing? Am I making it?" Jung calls this person the introvert. His meaning is somewhat different from the common use of the word. Jung defines the introvert as a power-oriented person who wants to put through his own internal image of how things should be.

The sex-oriented person, on the other hand, turns outward. Falling in love means losing yourself in another object. This person Jung calls the extrovert. Now, he says, every individual is both, with an accent on one or the other. If you have your accent 60 percent over in the power arena, it's only going to be 40 percent over in the *eros* area.

Now, when you run into a situation where your normal orientation doesn't function, where it isn't carrying you through, you are thrown back on the secondary drive. Then this inferior personality emerges. The characteristic of the inferior personality is compulsiveness—you can't control yourself, your voice quivers, you blush, you get angry, and so forth. You are out of control; the inferior character has taken over. It is more primitive than the developed side of the personality.

Jung uses a fine word for this reversal: he calls it an enantiodromia. As you know (of course) from your Greek, *dromia* is "to run": *hippodrome* is where the hippos (or horses) run; a *dromedary* is a racing camel. *Enantio* means "in the other direction." So, taken together, *enantiodromia* means "running in the opposite direction," turning turtle.

Now, the interesting thing about middle life is that, quite often, a chronic enantiodromia takes place. You have been, let us say, a power man: you've had it all, you have achieved what you set out to achieve, or at least your wits have been about you, and you've realized it isn't worth achieving.

When that moment comes, the change takes place. You have disposable libido, available libido, and where does it go? It goes over there to the twinkle-twinkle side, and Papa begins to see the little girls. Then everybody asks, "What has happened to Daddy?" This is the normal phenomenon of the nervous breakdown in late middle age. A gentleman has gained all the power in the world, and he's had this image of retirement: "I'm going to retire and go fishing." Of course that's what he wants, because fishing was what he was in love with when he was eleven years old. This is Daddy and his quest for mermaids that I talked about before.

For an example of the opposite reversal—from sex to the power drive—just take the woman who has been the mother of a family. Perhaps she's had several lovers, but she now has grandchildren and recollections of lovely dance engagements and all this kind of thing. At this point, she becomes a power monster: the fabulous mother-in-law whom I also mentioned earlier. Her children, whom she's brought up, are beginning to leave. The whole sense of loss—of power inferiority—washes over her. She has to grab on and tell them to shut the window, open the window, put the baby in the bath, take the baby out of the bath, do this, do that. Of course, she is completely compulsive about it. It's a fantastic and frightening thing to have your second, hidden side come up.

Now, I'm overplaying it; this is a diagrammatic approach, let us grant. Yet even so, almost everyone faces this kind of crisis. The problem is, when this enantiodromia comes, are you going to be able to absorb and integrate the other factor, the other side of your personality?

Jung calls the problem of this so-called midlife crisis *integration:* the integration of the two sides of the personality in terms of an individual culture experience. Jung's whole approach to psychology is based on the idea of these interactions.

Remember, Freud explored the idea of the wish and the prohibition, essentially a collision between the psychological and the sociological. Jung believed that the collision is intrinsic to the individual's psyche; that is to say, every time you stress one side, the other side loses. In Wagner's *Ring,* Albrecht gets the ring of power by spurning the allure of the Rhine maidens—that's the power man, right there. The other man, over on the opposite side, would say, "I don't want to make history, I just want to make love." But someday it'll dawn on him, "Hey, I didn't make history." The terrible thing about this enantiodromia is that it is filled with the echo of "too late." In this way, past decisions assume seemingly disastrous proportions.

Now, there's more to a person than simply sex and power. Jung sees the psyche as dominated by what he calls four functions, divided into two opposing pairs.

Jung calls the first duad sensibility (or feeling) and intellect. There are two ways of analyzing what you perceive around you. You can base your life on evaluating things by how they feel; then you will have a wonderfully differentiated and developed sensibility. Your appreciation of the arts and the nuances and the richness of life will be great. On the other hand, you can judge things in terms of intellectual decisions—right and wrong, propitious and unpropitious, prudent and imprudent. If you make your decisions on only one basis, the other is not being developed.

In Jung's experience dealing with Occidentals—this may or may not be true for all cultures—the society requires men to develop the thinking, intellectual function, while it requires women to develop the feeling function, sensibility.

Of course, whichever function isn't stressed takes on an inferior quality. Inferior thinking might be called mere opinion. They used to say, "You can't argue with a woman." Well, you can't argue with a woman whose perception has been primarily developed in terms of feeling functions; her decisions do not come from logical connections, and she may have a whole system of opinions that are based on feeling rather than actually thinking anything through. If a young man had any idea about the maturity and sophistication of the "feeling" that was sitting across the table from him while he's being a slob, he would be completely surprised.[35]

Inferior feeling is sentimentalism. We all know what that means. The sentiments of a cruel man, or a man who leads his life purely as a scientist without any thought of feelings, are grossly undeveloped. When he does come forth with sentiment, the kind of books or plays or music he likes will tend to be thin and trite; they're no good at all.

It is the dialogue between these two functions that educates us. The inferior function—whether intellect or sensibility—remains in the unconscious. When it comes up, it comes up compulsively; it can't be argued with. So these two are sides that have to be developed; one will be inferior and the other superior. This works like the sex and power balance, but it is a totally different matter; sex and power, for our purposes, are unrelated.

The other duad offers two ways of having an experience: Jung calls the first way sensation (different from feeling); he calls the other way intuition (also different from feeling). Here we are, sitting in a room, bombarded by sights, sounds, smells, tastes, and so forth. What is here in the room comes to us through our sensation; sensation relates us to the space around us.

A student comes into the room. You try to discover the student's capacities, why that student came into the room, and what he is likely to do. This is intuition. Intuition is the primary political talent. It is the tact for time, the sense of the possible. The intuitive person sees the future and past stretching out like ribbons of probability.

Again, one function will be superior and the other inferior. If you always live in terms of the potentialities of things—the intuitive realities—then you're not living in terms of the actualities, the sensual realities. And, of course, vice versa. Once again, at some point in your life, the inferior function will come to the forefront, and it will threaten you when it does.

Now, instead of simply going into the forest when middle age hits and canceling the whole darn show, as in the Indian tradition, Jung says the Occidental approach to the transition from responsibility to old age is that of achieving wholeness, of *individuation*. This is exactly the Greek idea. He felt you have to balance out these competing functions—sex versus power, intellect versus sensibility, intuition versus sensation—in order to escape the enantiodromia of the midlife crisis. So, as a child, you begin as a whole thing, then certain functions develop more than others, and you are a part thing throughout your social, mature working life, and, finally, in the last stage, you become a whole thing again. You go to an adult education program or something like that, which helps to preserve the sensibility while you're working on the intellect.

The Archetypes of the Collective Unconscious

These polarities—the two attitudes and four functions—are all interior, psychological dynamics. They flow through our psyches like ocean tides. Within the mind, Jung also identified certain fixed structures. These structures aren't learned, Freudian introjections. In Jung's view, they are there from our birth. They evolved as a part of the human mind, just as the hand or eye evolved. Like the hand and eye, almost all of us share these structures in common. He therefore called them the archetypes of the collective unconscious. By *collective,* he meant nothing metaphysical; he was merely referring to what he saw as their commonality among all human beings.

The first of these structures Jung called the self. For Jung, the self encompasses all of the possibilities of your life, the energies, the potentialities—everything that you are capable of becoming. The total self is what your life would be if it were entirely fulfilled.

Jung regards the total potential of the individual's psyche as an entity. Jung describes the self as a circle, its center unknown to you. That center, which is deep in the unconscious mind, is pushing you, your capacities, and your instincts. It gradually wakes during the first part of your life and gradually goes to sleep again in later stages. This is going on in you, and you have no control over it.

Now, this self opens out into nature and the universe because it is simply a part of nature. Yet the particular body has particular capacities, organs, and incapacities, commits you to a certain mode of experiencing that great consciousness of which you are an instrument. So your self will be peculiar to you, and yet it will be simply a local inflection of the model; you have a particular realization and sensibility of the great mystery. As you act as an infant, you are impelled by that self. This is the instinct system operating, purely biological.

The young girl in adolescence—and I taught them for thirty-eight years at Sarah Lawrence—is simply startled at what a wonderful thing she is. She didn't *do* it, but whenever she looks in the mirror, she sees the miracle of something that happened to her that is called by her name. Here is this thing that comes into being. This is the whole flower of the self. But our little consciousness rides on top of that like a ship on an ocean.

As you become aware of your self, your ego comes into birth. In Jung's schema, the ego is your conscious identification with your particular body, its experiences, and its memories. Memory and experience, limited to a body and identified in terms of the temporal continuity of that body, of which you are consciously aware: this is the ego.

By the time you've learned to walk and talk, write and drive, you've already got a lot of wishes of which you are unconscious, but because you have never fulfilled them or not kept your mind on them, they've fallen into the depths of the self, into the unconscious. The self is the whole context of potentials. The ego is your consciousness of your self, what you think you are, what you think you're capable of, and it's blocked by all of these unconsciously retained memories of incapacity, prohibitions, and so forth.

So, you have a dawning consciousness; you can watch this awakening in a little baby as it begins to realize itself as ego. The self and ego are not the same. The ego is the center of conscious mind only; it encompasses your awareness of your self and your world.

Now, when your ego has a plan, and you commit some absurd fumble that breaks the plan up, it's as though someone had intruded and destroyed your plan. You're interrupting yourself; you forgot something. Freud dealt with this very well; this semi-intentional forgetting is now known as a Freudian slip. You are simply keeping yourself from doing what you only thought you wanted to do. The other side of you is talking. This is coming from that unconscious aspect of the self. The self is the totality, and if you think of it as a circle, the center of the circle would be the center of the self. But your plane of consciousness is above the center, and your ego's up above that plane of consciousness, so there's a subliminal aspect of the self of which you do not know. And that is in play constantly with the ego.

Now, Jung's is a slightly different definition of ego from Freud's, though it is related. For Jung, ego is your notion of your self. It defines the center of your consciousness and relates you to the world; it is the "I" you experience as acting on the world around you.

It has nothing to do, however, with the unconscious portion of the self. The ego normally stays above the line of consciousness. Now, suppose you're driving a car: you're on the left side of the road, at the wheel; meanwhile, you don't know that there's another side there. In fact, you don't even recognize that you're on one side; you think you're in the middle. Most people drive their lives in this way, according to Jung. They think their ego is who they are. They go driving that way, and, of course, the car is knocking people down on the other side of the road. How are you going to enable yourself to see that other side? Do you put another wheel up and have a friend drive you? Do you put the wheel in the middle? No! You have to know what's over there; you have to learn to see three-dimensionally, to use the parallax principle.

So, we have the self, which is the total potentiality, you might say. You have the ego, which emerges gradually in the course of childhood to a comparatively firm notion of itself. Until that ego is more or less confirmed, it is very dangerous to have experiences that the ego can't handle. It can be blown, and you lose the ego's grip on conscious reality entirely. Then you're in a schizophrenic condition. You've got to have your ego in play.

We hear so much talk now, particularly from the Orient, about egolessness. You are trying to smash this thing which is the only thing that keeps you in play. There's got to be somebody up there; otherwise you're not oriented to anything. The self, that's the great circle, the ship, and the ego is the little captain on the bridge.

Now, as you grow up, your family says you belong to this social circle, and you must behave as we do here. Then you go to school, and you begin to find that there's a certain career dawning, a certain kind of life you're going to lead. This begins tightening you down. In other words, the circumstances of the society in which you are living are beginning to force you into a certain role, a certain costume.

There are certain things the ego must learn to do in order to function in the society you live in. There's no point in learning to live in a society that does not exist or that lives over on the other side of the Iron Curtain. This which you have around you is it, my friend.

And the first problem of the early stage of life is to learn to live in this society in a way that will relate you to the objective world in terms that make sense now. The critical function can come a little later, but first you've got to learn to function here and now. And this is the great task of childhood and youth: the terror, the demands, the restrictions of your will, and so forth have to be faced and assimilated. If you avoid these challenges early on, you will simply have to face them later or go slithering along, partially realized as a human entity, never having had the experiences of playing in a serious situation.

Society has a number of roles it needs us to play. We assume these roles just as an actor might slip into the different pieces of a costume. Society imprints on us its ideals, a wardrobe of acceptable behavior. Jung calls these personae. *Persona* is the Latin word for the mask worn by an actor on the stage.

Say you're a teacher: when you're at work, you put on a teacher mask—you are a Teacher. Suppose you go home and think you're still a Teacher, not just a fellow who teaches. Who would want to be around you?

Sometimes, in high school dramatics, some poor kid plays the role of Hamlet, and his aunt tells him he did it wonderfully. Well, he's Hamlet from then on. He's identified himself with the role.

There are other people who find that they have become, to their own amazement perhaps, executives. They are executives at the office. They are executives when they are at home. They are executives when they go to bed—which is disappointing to their spouses.

The mask has to be left in the wardrobe, in the green room, as it were. You've got to know what play you're in at any one time. You've got to be able to separate your sense of yourself—your ego—from the self you show the rest of the world—your persona.

You find this first big tension within the psyche between the dark inner potential of the self's unconscious portions on the one hand and the persona system on the other. The ego learns about the outside and inside and tries to reconcile them.

Now, one of the great dangers, from Jung's standpoint, is to identify yourself with your persona. In dramatic contrast to the aim of education in the Orient, Jung declares the ego must distinguish itself from its role.

This is a concept that does not exist in the East. As Freud put it, the ego is that function which puts you in touch with the empirical actualities of the world in which you live; it is the reality function. And it's from developing ego that you develop your own value system. Your judgments, your critical faculties, and so forth are functions of your ego. In the Orient, the individual is asked not to develop his critical faculties, not to observe the world in a new way, but to accept without question the teaching of his guru and to assume the mask that the society puts on him. This is the fundamental law of karmic birth. You are born into exactly that role which is proper to you. The society will give you the mask to wear. You are to identify with it completely, canceling out every creative thought.

In traditional India, China, or Japan, you *are* your role. The secret is to embody that role perfectly, whether as a mendicant monk or a grieving widow throwing herself on the pyre. You are to become *satī*.

What Jung says is that you should play your role, knowing that it's *not you*. It's a quite different point of view. This requires individuation, separating your ego, your image of yourself, from the social role. This doesn't mean that you shouldn't play the social role; it simply means that no matter what you choose to do in life, whether it's to cop out or to cop in, you are playing a role, and don't take it too damned seriously. The persona is merely the mask you're wearing for this game.

The people who know best how to change roles are Occidental women. They dress in a different costume and step into a transformed personality. My wife, who is a dancer, is a past master at this. She's much inclined to be very cold when it's snowy. But when she dresses with almost nothing on and goes out in the middle of the winter to a party, she does not shiver at all. She is completely there; her whole personality has put itself into the role—and voilà.

It goes even further than this, because the whole persona complex includes your moral principles. Ethics and social mores are internalized as part of the persona order, and Jung tells us that you must take that lightly, too. Just remember, Adam and Eve fell when they learned the difference between good and evil. So the way to get back is *not* to know the difference. That's an obvious lesson, but it's not one that's very clearly preached from pulpits. Yet Christ told his disciples, "Judge not, that ye be not judged."[36] You judge according to your persona context, and you will be judged in terms of it. Unless you can learn to look beyond the local dictates of what is right and what is wrong, you're not a complete human being. You're just a part of that particular social order.

So, here we have the self with all the potentialities. You have a growing ego consciousness with which you identify yourself, and this is developing in relation to the costumes you have to put on, the personae. It's good to have a lot of costumes, so long as each costume fits your conscience. The moral order is part of your persona.

There's a lot in you that's neither being carried into this persona system nor into your ego, as part of what you perceive as "you." Just opposite to the ego, buried in the unconscious, is what Jung calls the shadow.

Now, the society will give you a role to play, and this means that you've got to cut out of your life many of the things that you, as a person, might think or do. These potentials get shunted down into the unconscious. Your society tells you, "You should do this, you should do that"; but it also says, "You mustn't do this, you mustn't do the other thing." Those things you'd like to do, which are really not very nice things to want to do, those get placed down in the unconscious, too. This is the center of the personal unconscious.

The shadow is, so to say, the blind spot in your nature. It's that which you won't look at about yourself. This is the counterpart exactly of the Freudian unconscious, the repressed recollections as well as the repressed potentialities in you.

The shadow is that which you might have been had you been born on the other side of the tracks: the other person, the other you. It is made up of the desires and ideas within you that you are repressing—all of the introjected id. The shadow is the landfill of the self. Yet it is also a sort of vault: it holds great, unrealized potentialities within you.

The nature of your shadow is a function of the nature of your ego. It is the backside of your light side. In the myths, the shadow is represented as the monster that has to be overcome, the dragon. It is the dark thing that comes up from the abyss and confronts you the minute you begin moving down into the unconscious. It is the thing that scares you so that you don't want to go down there. It knocks from below. Who's that down there? Who's that up there? This is all very, very mysterious and frightening.

If your personal role is too thin, too narrow—if you've buried too much of yourself within your shadow—you're going to dry up. Most of your energies are not available to you. A lot can get gathered there in the depths. And eventually, enantiodromia is going to hit, and that unrecognized, unheeded demon is going to come roaring up into the light.

The shadow is the part of you that you don't know is there. Your friends see it, however, and it's also why some people don't like you. The shadow is you as you might have been; it is that aspect of you which might have been if you had allowed yourself to fulfill your unacceptable potential.

Society, of course, does not recognize these aspects of your potential self. You are not recognizing these aspects of yourself either; you don't know that they're there or that you have repressed them.

If you think of the self as a great circle with a center, and you think of consciousness as well above that center, then the ego is up in the center of consciousness, and the shadow would be way down opposite in the deep unconscious. The shadow is interred down there for a reason; it is that aspect of yourself that your ego doesn't know about, which you bury because it doesn't fit how you perceive yourself to be. The shadow is that part of you that you won't allow to show through, that includes good—I mean potent—as well as dangerous and disastrous aspects of your potential.

Now, typically, all these archetypes come out personified in myths and dreams. We personify the mystery of the universe as God. The ego becomes the hero or heroine figure. The unconscious self becomes the wise man or woman. The shadow becomes personified, too, as a kind of Mephistophelian figure. Evidently, the shadow holds not only what is good for you but what is bad as well. It swallows those things that it would be dangerous for you to express, such as the murderous intent that you have for that son of a gun over there who's been interrupting you all evening, the urge to steal, to cheat, to destroy, and so on. But it also holds potentialities that your ego and the persona system don't want to accept.

In your dreams, and in the myths of your society, these urges are represented in the shadow, and the shadow is always of your own sex; it is always to be seen as a threat.

You can recognize who it is by simply thinking of the people you don't like. They correspond to that person whom you might have been—otherwise they wouldn't mean very much to you. People who excite you either positively or negatively have caught something projected from yourself:

> I do not love thee, Dr. Fell.
> The reason why I cannot tell,
> But this alone I know full well,
> I do not love thee, Dr. Fell.[37]

Why? Because he's my shadow. I don't know whether you've had similar experiences in your life, but there are people I despise the minute I see them. These people represent those aspects of myself, the existence of which I refuse to admit to myself. The ego tends to identify itself with the society, forgetting this shadow. It thinks it's you. That's the position society puts us in. Society does not give a darn whether you crack up when it's through with you—that's your problem.

I remember hearing one clergyman say to me, "If I didn't believe in God and Christ and the Church, I would be a terrible person." Well, I said, "What do you think you'd do?" He couldn't think. I said, "I bet I can tell you what you think you'd do, but I won't tell you. All I can tell you is you'd get tired pretty soon, and you'd find you're just another old drag in the world, and you wouldn't have blown it up at all. And even if you did blow up some little portion of it, that would soon be built up and you would have been no great menace to the world. So let yourself go. Do some of those things. You'd find that they're not all so bad at all either, and you won't be saying things like that anymore."

You should find a way to realize your shadow in your life somehow.

Next comes the problem of gender. Every man has to be a manly man, and all of the things that society doesn't allow him to develop he attributes to the feminine side. These parts of himself he represses in his unconscious. This is the counterplayer to the persona. They become what Jung calls the anima: the female ideal in the masculine unconscious.

Likewise, the woman carries the animus in her unconscious: the male aspect in herself. She's a woman, and the society gives her certain things to do. All that is in her that she has associated with the masculine mode of life is repressed within the animus.

The interesting thing is that—biologically and psychologically—we have both sexes in us; yet in all human societies, one is allowed to accent only one. The other is internalized within us. Furthermore, our imagery and notions of the other are functions of our biography. This biography includes two aspects. One is general to the human species: nearly everybody has a mother and a father. The other aspect is peculiar to yourself: that your mother should have been as she was and your father as he was. There is a specification of the male and female roles as experienced, and this has committed, has determined, the quality of our experience of these great, great bases which everyone experiences. Everyone experiences Mother; everyone experiences Father.

In both cases, the buried ideal tends to be projected outward. We usually call this reaction falling in love: projecting your own ideal for the opposite sex onto some person who, by some kind of magnetism, causes your anima/animus to emerge. Now, you can go to a dance and there's some perfectly decent, nice-looking girl who's sitting all alone. Then there's some other little bumblebee with everybody all around her. What's she got? Well, it's something about the way her eyes are set that just evokes anima projections from all the males in the neighborhood. There are ways to present yourself that way; yet we don't always know what they are or how to achieve them. I've seen people who are perfectly good anima objects so make themselves up that they repel the anima projection.

Two people meet and fall in love. Then they marry, and the real Sam or Suzy begins to show through the fantasy, and, boy, is it a shock. So a lot of little boys and girls just withdraw their anima or animus. They get a divorce and wait for another receptive person, pitch the woo again, and, uh-oh, another shock. And so on and so forth.

Now the one undeniable fact: this disillusion is inevitable. You had an ideal. You married that ideal, then along comes a fact that doesn't correspond to that ideal. You suddenly notice things that don't quite fit with your projection. So what are you going to do when that happens? There's only one attitude that will solve the situation: compassion. This poor, poor fact that I married does not correspond to my ideal; it's only a human being. Well, I'm a human being, too. So I'll meet a human being for a change; I'll live with it and be nice to it, showing compassion for the fallibilities that I myself have certainly brought to life as a human being.

Perfection is inhuman. Human beings are not perfect. What evokes our love—and I mean love, not lust—is the imperfection of the human being. So, when the imperfection of the real person, compared to the ideal of your animus or anima, peeks through, say, This is a challenge to my compassion. Then make a try, and something might begin to get going here. You might begin to be quit of your fix on your anima. It's just as bad to be fixed on your anima and miss as to be fixed on your persona: you've got to get free of that. And the lesson of life is to release you from it. This is what Jung calls individuation, to see people and yourself in terms of what you indeed are, not in terms of all these archetypes that you are projecting around and that have been projected on you.

Of course, Saint Paul says, "Love beareth all things," but you may not be equal to God.[38] To expect too much compassion from yourself might be a little destructive of your own existence. Even so, at least make a try, and this goes not only for individuals but also for life itself. It's so easy. It's a fashionable idiocy of youth to say the world has not come up to your expectations. "What? I was coming, and this is all they could prepare for me?" Throw it out. Have compassion for the world and those in it. Not only political life but all life stinks, and you must embrace that with compassion.

In his early novel *Tonio Kröger,* Thomas Mann has given us the answer of what to do when reality shines through the projected mask.[39] He tells the story of a young man who discovers this fact, this need for compassion. In the novel, Tonio Kröger is born in northern Germany, into a town where everybody was blue-eyed and blond and healthy and strong and at ease with their particular world. They were incarnations, you might say, of the persona. Tonio's mother was Italian or of Mediterranean birth. His very name tells you what a mixed-up mess he is. He is dark-eyed and dark-haired and has inherited a certain nervous sensibility that makes him potentially an artist and writer. Although he's devoted to these blond, here-and-now people, he can't play with them; he's in the observer's position all the time. He does, however, see how wonderful they are. When he goes to dances, they're wonderful to watch: the girls dance so well. The boys dance so well. And when he dances, he thinks, I want just to dream and she wants just to dance. And the girls he gets are the ones who fall down when they dance. And so he finds himself on the outside.

When he grows up a bit, he decides he's going to be an artist, he's going away; he's going to another world. So he heads south, probably to Munich, and gets involved in a bohemian community there, in what we would call a hippie community. And there he finds people who have great ideals about what life should be; along with that, they have a wonderful vocabulary of incrimination through which they devalue everything that actually is doing well in the world. These are people who have a lot of ideas and find that the world doesn't live up to those ideas and who have withdrawn their projection, their love for the world, and been disillusioned by it. They're cold, they're disdainful, and they're cynical. Tonio finds that this doesn't work for him, either. He's an intellectual, too, he respects ideas, but he does love those blue-eyed blonds.

Tonio is a young man who is stuck between two worlds: the world of unimaginative doers that he was born into and the world of intellectual bohemian critics with whom he has been wandering. He ultimately discovers that anybody who is in the world is imperfect, and that imperfection is what keeps the person here. He realizes that nothing alive fits the ideal. If you are going to describe a person as an artist, you must describe the person with ruthless objectivity. It is the imperfections that identify them. It is the imperfections that ask for our love.

The thing that turns what Mann calls a *litterateur*—that's a person who writes for a New York magazine, say—into a poet or an artist, a person who can give humanity the images to help it live, is that the artist recognizes the imperfections around him with compassion. The principle of compassion is that which converts disillusionment into a participatory companionship. So when the fact shows through the animus or anima, what you must render is compassion. This is the basic love, the charity, that turns a critic into a living human being who has something to give to—as well as to demand of—the world.

This is how one is to deal with animus and anima disillusionment. This disappointment will evoke. That's reality evoking a new depth of reality in yourself, because you're imperfect, too. You may not know it. The world is a constellation of imperfections, and you, perhaps, are the most imperfect of all. By your love for the world you name it accurately and without pity and love what you have thus named. Mann calls this opposition erotic irony. This discovery can help you save your marriage.

So, what have we got? We have the self, which is this great unwritten page. We have the ego, which is a consciousness becoming gradually more and more expanded in its field of experience and light. We have the persona, which is the field of the *Völkergedanken,* the local, ethnic way of living life. If the imagery of the society doesn't bring your unconscious into play in its conscious world, you have a kind of dead situation; you become lost in a wasteland.

Among the archetypes, the first to turn threatening is the shadow. That's what you're holding down, and holding that down has made you capable of living the life that the society wills you to live.

The next challenge is the opposite sex. And here is the great fascination. Freud was certainly right here. Particularly in puberty, the allure and mystery of life are epitomized in the quality of the opposite sex.

Now comes the great psychological thing. One falls in love at first sight. Now, what in heaven's name does that mean? You don't even know the person. Everybody, I hope, has had the experience. Somebody walks in the room, and your heart stops.

Thomas Mann writes some beautiful examples of this. In his first published story, "Der Kleine Herr Friedmann," the little gentleman of the title has a cathartic experience. He's a funny little fellow, and he has never been able in one way or another to get into relationship to life at all. One day, this gorgeous, statuesque blonde appears. And what does he say? "My God, my God." The heart has stopped, and he has realized that he has not lived life. The world has opened up. This is the appearance of the guiding anima.[40]

Now, whether you like it or not, that's going to work on you. Well, one of the boldest things you could possibly do would be to marry that ideal that you've fallen for. Then you face a real job, because everything has been projected onto him or her. This goes beyond lust; this is something that goes way down. It pulls everything out. This anima/animus is the fish line that has caught your whole unconscious, and everything's going to come up—the Midgard Serpent, everything down in the bottom. This is what you marry.

There was a gentleman who has since become a Jungian analyst. This chap told Dr. Jung of a dream. In it there was a great cliff, and over the cliff there came the head of a serpent. The serpent came down—and it was enormous—it came down, and down, and it just seemed endless. And Jung said, "That's Miss So-and-so. Marry her." And the chap did. It was a very happy marriage.

But what goes on when you marry this love-at-first-sight situation? Well, what you have married is a projection. You have married something that has been projected from yourself: the mask that you've put over the other person.

What is the sensible thing to do in a circumstance like this? What is the pedagogically advisable thing to do in a situation like this? What shows itself through the mask of the projection is a fact. The mask is your ideal. This fact does not coincide with the ideal; it is imperfect. What do you do about what is imperfect?

Jung believed that the idea is to reject all projections. Not to identify the women you meet with your anima projection. Not to identify yourself with your persona projection. To release all projections and ideals. This is what Jung means by individuation. Jung calls the individual who identifies himself with his persona a *mana* personality; we would call him a stuffed shirt. That's a person who is nothing but the role he or she plays. A person of this sort never lets his actual character develop. He remains simply a mask, and as his powers fail—as he makes mistakes and so forth—he becomes more and more frightened of himself, puts more and more of an effort into keeping up the mask. Then the separation between the persona and the self takes place, forcing the shadow to retreat further and further into the abyss.

You are to assimilate the shadow, embrace it. You don't have to act on it, necessarily, but you must know it and accept it.

You are not to assimilate the anima/animus—that's a different challenge. You are to relate to it through the other.

The only way one can become a human being is through relationships to other human beings. And they will be male or female, and you will be an other, too. The males will always have, for the female, animus associations, one way or the other, and the females for the male, anima associations.

And the first way is that of compassion. This is not desire. This is not fear. Buddha, Christ, and the rest have made it very clear that we've got to get past those two.

Now, when you go down into the unconscious, you're pulling up not only the shadow and anima, but also those faculties for experiencing and judging that have not been employed in your life. You come to integrate the inferior functions and attitudes, so that any enantiodromia is merely a matter of realizing your full potential, not a wreck on the Sirens' rocks.

There are four kinds of crisis that can bring about a very serious enantiodromia. One is that you have passed from one life stage to another and you didn't know it—the late-middle-aged gentleman who's obsessed about his golf score and has not moved into the phase of the later half of life.

Jung says life is like the day of a solar journey. The first part of it is up, moving from birth to the society. And the second part of it is down, moving from participation in the world and the society to death. And whereas the threat of the first half of life was life, the threat of the second half is death, and all the symbols are changing meaning.

Through the remaining part of life, Jung says, the great problem is integrating the inferior with the superior functions. That's the great task of your later years. So let's just think of the imagery of the union of opposites. The same symbol that for an extrovert will have sexual content, for an introvert will resonate with battle. Once one begins to reach individuation and integration, one finds the conjunction of those two aspects of one's own psyche.

The crisis of passing from one life stage to another without being ready to move on arrests this process. This is the difficulty for the forty-year-old infant and for the sixty-year-old who thinks he is still thirty-five. Life brought you up to the solar apex, then it began to curve—and you think you're still up at the peak? Oh, no, boy. You're way down here. And what a drop you're going to have. Much better to know when you've started down and enjoy the ride; there are nice things down here, too.

The second kind of crisis is a relaxation of life requirements. You worked like hell to become the shoelace czar of the universe. You own every shoelace factory in the world. And now, at the age of forty-odd, you don't have to put that energy into it anymore. The thing's going all by itself, and you've got secretaries who are not only taking the job in hand but also looking a little better to you than you thought little girls should look, and suddenly there's a lot of distraction. You have all of this disposable libido. And where does it go?

The eros-oriented extrovert turns around and suddenly becomes a power monster. Good old Uncle Harry, the shoelace king, the introverted power man, becomes an old lecher—that kind of thing. But the tragedy about this crisis is the deep sense that it's all too late. Nothing is as it should be, and it's because you're doing the wrong thing.

Another kind of crisis is the loss of confidence in your moral ideals; this form of enantiodromia is something that one finds often among young people in college. The young person is living with a roommate who comes from another order of society altogether, either the poor person who's living with the wealthy or the wealthy with the poor, or the Christian with the atheist, or the Jew with the Buddhist. You find out that here is a perfectly decent person also. It's not that the other person seduces you into sin; it's that getting to know them makes you question your own moral principles. And since those moral principles—the persona complex—are holding your ego in place, when they relax all the rest comes out. There's the threat or the allure of becoming a terrible person: what I call the knock knock of the shadow from underneath. That's your own dark person talking. You might also get what I call the twinkle twinkle of the anima/animus: come, little boy, it's interesting around the corner. You've never seen girls like this.

Well, says Jung, let it come. Let it go. But don't do it with such abandon that your ego is entirely shattered. Imagine one of my college students. She's had her first few classes in a sociology course, and she discovers that her father's fortune is built on blood and bones. She goes home for the Thanksgiving dinner, and the family wonders what has happened. The student begins coming to her conferences and classes looking like a wreck. She lets her hair go. She has gone over to the other side. She has tipped over. It's enantiodromia. She has assumed partisanship for the opposite side— she's waving the banner of the downtrodden proletariat. And that's just as extreme as being on the side she was on before, in blissful ignorance.

Well, it's not a bad thing to happen, because you do get to experience all that's over on the other side. It's just like the underside of the rug coming up. In fact, my students sometimes looked a bit like the underside of a rug. And it's good to have a thing like that happen in an institution like a college, where you can somewhat protect the person, because the idea is, eventually, to integrate the two halves.

Now, there's one other crisis, and this is a very serious challenge: the intolerable decision where you really have to do something that you regard as immoral, beneath your dignity, something you're totally ashamed of. The great example, of course, is Abraham's sacrifice of Isaac. The voice of God invited him to kill his son, and he faced an impossible decision. He was forced either to disobey what he took to be God or to kill his son. If he didn't sacrifice Isaac, he would have disobeyed God, and if he did kill Isaac, he would have violated the first principle of human decency. Fathers should not kill their sons.

Well, this is an intolerable decision. And intolerable decisions may meet you. I had friends during the Depression who had families and no jobs; they had to do some things that they would not, as people in charge of their own lives, have wished to do for the maintenance of their families. These are the sorts of things that bust up your ego and bring up the whole content of the unconscious.

Now the problem of individuation for Jung, the challenge of the middle-life crisis, lies in cutting these projections loose. When you realize that moral ideals—the moral life to which you are supposed to be committed—are embodied in the persona, you realize the depth and threat of this psychology. You are to put your morals on and take them off according to propriety, the propriety of the moment; you are *not* to identify these morals with cosmic truths. The laws of society, therefore, are social conventions, not eternal laws, and they are to be handled and judged in terms of their appropriateness to what they are intended to do. The individual makes his own judgment as to how he acts. Then he has to look out to be sure that the guardians of the social order do not misunderstand or make things difficult for him because he is not totally playing their game. But the main problem of integration is to find relationships to the outside world and to live a rich life in full play.

In effect, the individual must learn to live by his or her own myth.

CHAPTER V

PERSONAL MYTH

JUNG: WHAT MYTH DO I LIVE BY?

For many, many years I've been speaking about mythology in rather an abstract way—how it was here, how it was there—and it seems to be about time that I accepted the challenge to say something about how it might be for you and for me. Now, this topic of living your own, personal myth—finding it, learning what it is, and riding on it—first occurred to me when I read Jung's autobiographical work *Memories, Dreams, Reflections*. In one passage, he describes a crisis in his own life. In 1911–12, Jung was working on his seminal book *The Symbols of Transformation*.

He was tremendously upset at that time because he had come to feel that all of his earlier work had been on the basis of a superficial understanding of the psychology of his deeply psychotic patients. He had begun his career working at the Burghölzli Sanitarium in Zürich under Eugen Bleuler. Bleuler was the man who coined the term *schizophrenia,* and a great many of the patients in his sanitarium were, in fact, schizophrenic.

It was after he had worked there for some time and had already received his doctorate under Bleuler that Jung became acquainted with Freud. Now, Freud's principal concern was with neurotics. A neurotic is a

85

person who is still functioning in the world with a working, conscious orientation to life, but who is troubled by an inadequate relationship to the unconscious system. A psychotic, on the other hand, is someone who is cracked off entirely. And Jung, working with the psychotics, had become pretty well acquainted with what might be called the archetypology of unconscious imagination.

He began reading books on comparative myth: Frobenius, Bastian, Frazer. The realization came to him that the imagery that his patients were finding welling up from their own psyches was precisely that with which the world of comparative mythologists and their history of religion studies were already familiar. The imagery of his patients' fantasizing showed precise parallels to mythological themes. Jung then noticed that the parallels held true not only with psychotics but with neurotics and with relatively well-balanced people as well.

This discovery impressed him tremendously and motivated him to immerse himself in the study of mythology. *Symbols of Transformation,* which deals with the interrelationship between dream consciousness and the mythological consciousness of visions, was the very book that made it impossible for Freud to work with Jung anymore. It made it clear that Jung no longer believed that sex was the beginning, middle, and end of the subconscious symbolic system, and that regressive psychoanalysis was the only therapy. To Freud and his followers, this was anathema.

When Jung finished this book, it did not mark the end of his insights on the topic. "Hardly had I finished the manuscript," he says in *Memories, Dreams, Reflections,* "when it struck me what it means to live with a myth, and what it means to live without one. . . ."[41] It occurred to him to ask himself by what myth he himself was living, and he realized he did not know. "So, in the most natural way, I took it upon myself to get to know my myth, and this I regarded as my task of tasks."[42]

It's my belief that there is no longer a single mythology operating for everybody in any one country, let alone across Western civilization. It's my notion that the social order today is essentially secular in character. It does not claim its laws to have been divinely given. We don't explain our laws in mythological terms. In the old days, the laws were delivered by God to Moses and laid out in the Books of Numbers, Deuteronomy, and Leviticus. We don't have that. Even the laws of the physical universe, as I've said, are less than fixed. We don't know. We keep finding out new things about it, but we don't have a deliberate image of the universe that's going to stick for very long.

With respect to the development of each individual's psychology, we have such varied sources from which we've come and such varied opportunities in our lives that there is no single mythology that can have it for us. My belief is that within the field of a secular society, which is a sort of neutral frame that allows individuals to develop their own lives, so long as they don't annoy their neighbors too much, each of us has an individual myth that's driving us, which we may or may not know. That was the sense of Jung's question: what is the myth by which I am living?

I don't think that there is going to be anything like a unified mythology for mankind for a long time, if there ever is again. I think that our social life—that covered by the third function of myth—is now being handled in another, better way. I think, however, that the individual is left without a sense of his conscious and unconscious in communication with each other.

Mythological images are the images by which the consciousness is put in touch with the unconscious. That's what they are. When you don't have your mythological images, or when your consciousness rejects them for some reason or other, you are out of touch with your own deepest part. I think that's the purpose of a mythology that we can live by. We have to find the one that we are in fact living by and know what it is so that we can direct our craft with competence.

Now, many of us live by myths that guide us, myths that may prove adequate for our entire lives. For those who live by such myths, there's no problem here. They know what their myth is: one of the great inherited religious traditions or another. In all likelihood, this myth will suffice to guide them along the path of their lives.

There are others in this world, however, for whom these guideposts lead nowhere. You find these folks especially among university students, professors, people in the cities—the folks whom the Russians call the intelligentsia. For these, the old patterns and the old instructions just don't hold, so that when it comes to a life crisis, they are of no help.

There are others who may feel that they are living in accord with a certain system but actually are not. They go to church every Sunday and read the Bible, and yet those symbols aren't speaking to them. The driving power is coming from something else.

You might ask yourself this question: if I were confronted with a situation of total disaster, if everything I loved and thought I lived for were devastated, what would I live for? If I were to come home, find my family murdered, my house burned up, or all my career wiped out by some disaster or another, what would sustain me? We read about these things every day, and we think, Well, that only happens to other people. But what if it happened to me? What would lead me to know that I could go on living and not just crack up and quit?

I've known religious people who have had such experiences. They would say, "It is God's will." For them, faith would work.

Now, what do you have in your life that would play this role for you? What is the great thing for which you would sacrifice your life? What makes you do what you do; what is the call of your life to you—do you know it? The old traditions provided this mythic support for people; it held whole culture worlds together. Every great civilization has grown out of a mythic base.

In our day, however, there is great confusion. We're thrown back on ourselves, and we have to find that thing which, in truth, works for us as individuals. Now, how does one do this?

I think one of the great calamities of contemporary life is that the religions that we have inherited have insisted on the concrete historicity of their symbols. The Virgin Birth, for example, or the ascension into heaven—these are symbols that are found in the mythologies of the world. Their primary reference must be to the psyche from which they have come. They speak to us of something in ourselves. They cannot primarily refer to historical events. And one of the great problems that is confronting us now is that the authority of the institutions that have been presenting us with these symbols—the religions in which we have been raised—has come into doubt simply because they have insisted on talking about their underlying myths as historical events somewhere. The image of the Virgin Birth: what does it refer to? A historical, biological problem? Or is it a psychological, spiritual metaphor?[43]

I greatly admire the psychologist Abraham Maslow. As I was reading one of his books, however, I found a sort of value schedule, values that his psychological experiments had shown that people live for. He gave a list of five values: survival, security, personal relationships, prestige, and self-development. I looked at that list and I wondered why it should seem so strange to me. I finally realized that it struck me as strange because these are exactly the values that mythology transcends.

Survival, security, personal relationships, prestige, self-development—in my experience, those are exactly the values that a mythically inspired person *doesn't* live for. They have to do with the primary biological mode as understood by human consciousness. Mythology begins where madness starts. A person who is truly gripped by a calling, by a dedication, by a belief, by a zeal, will sacrifice his security, will sacrifice even his life, will sacrifice personal relationships, will sacrifice prestige, and will think nothing of personal development; he will give himself entirely to his myth. Christ gives you the clue when he says, "He that loseth his life for my sake shall find it."44

Maslow's five values are the values for which people live when they have nothing to live for. Nothing has seized them, nothing has caught them, nothing has driven them spiritually mad and made them worth talking to. These are the bores. (In a marvelous footnote to an essay on *Don Quixote,* Ortega y Gasset once wrote, "A bore is one who deprives us of our solitude without providing companionship."45)

The awakening of awe is the key here, what Leo Frobenius, the wonderful student of African cultures, called *Ergriffenheit,* being seized by something so that you are pulled out.

Now, it's not always easy or possible to know by what it is that you are seized. You find yourself doing silly things, and you have been seized but you don't know what the dynamics are. You have been struck by that awakening of awe, of fascination, of the experience of mystery—the awareness of your bliss. With that, you have the awakening of your mind in its own service. The brain can enable you to found a business in order to maintain your family and get you prestige in the community; given the right mind, it can do these things very well. But the brain can also impel you to give all that up because you become fascinated with some kind of mystery.

One of the most vivid examples I know of this phenomenon is the life of the French painter Paul Gauguin. He was a perfectly prosperous businessman with a family and a house; then he simply became fascinated by what began to open up for him in painting. You start doodling with things like painting and they might doodle you out of your life—that's what happened to Gauguin. He just went off on this adventure, forgot his family and everything else. His awakening led him to Tahiti and all of those beautiful paintings. He forgot all about Maslow's values and began simply to live his bliss.

When Jung said he wanted to find out what the myth was by which he was living, what he wanted to find out was what that unconscious or subliminal thing was that was making him do these peculiar, irrational things and giving him problems that his consciousness then had to resolve. So let us say now that it's with the awakening of awareness and the transcendence of the values that Abraham Maslow has announced here that our subject begins.

I've talked about *kuṇḍalinī* yoga, the Indian system that equates the spiritual development of the soul with a serpent's journey up through the body through seven stations, or *cakras.* The bottom three centers represent the survival drive, the sex drive, and the drive to power.

Now, the hierarchy of values that Maslow names corresponds to these bottom three *cakras.* These are values that we share with the animals. We have an animal body, though of course it's not the body of a dog or a gazelle, but the body of a human animal. And we live the animal life in the human mode. Let's not flatter ourselves into thinking that this is the highest aspect of our humanity. We want to hold on to life, just as animals do. We have sex urges, just as animals do. And we have the desire to win and defeat opposition and put down what's blocking us, just as animals do. And that sums up the hierarchy of values of Dr. Maslow.

When the *kuṇḍalinī* serpent reaches the fourth *cakra,* the soul experiences the awakening of awe, and in the Indian system, this is symbolized in the hearing of the sacred syllable *aum.* This is something animals don't hear. The apprehension of this sound opens a dimension of mystery into the universe, and the sense of wanting to understand that mystery is the beginning of the spiritual life. In the *kuṇḍalinī* system, the fourth *cakra* is at the level of the heart. It is at the heart, as they say, that the hands of the devotee touch the feet of the god. And it's only the feet of the god that you get at this level; you've got to go on up. So it's when that sense of mystery opens that we start.

Now, to give the animals their due, there is a little bit of this in the animals. Animals, at night when they see a light, will approach to know what it is. That's the beginning. In their next incarnation, they're going to be on the human level, you might say. This is the awakening of awe. But the light that we're now going to try to follow is going to lead finally to the pure, undifferentiated light of transcendence. That is the significance of the syllable *aum.*

So let us leave behind *cakras* one, two, and three, which have simply to do with the mundane, rational life. There's nothing to be said against them, because nobody will be there to experience the *aum* or the awe unless you have satisfied the survival needs. But they are merely the ground base of a larger structure, and we want to move up.

In the *kuṇḍalinī* system, the great human experience starts when *aum* is heard. Then the spirit is drawn to make the effort to get to know it more, to move in closer to it, and this urge is what is associated with the fifth *cakra,* which is at the level of the larynx, where the word begins, and this is where animals do not follow. They cannot speak. They can make sounds, but—so far as we know—no verbal communication, no concept communication.

With communication, the mystical experience begins.[46]

The beginning of a mythic world or a mythic tradition is a seizure—something that pulls you out of yourself, beyond yourself, beyond all rational patterns. It is out of such seizures that civilizations are built. All you have to do is look at their monuments, and you'll see that these are the nuttiest things that mankind ever thought of. Look at the Pyramids. Just try to interpret them in terms of rational means and aims or economic necessities; think of what it meant in a society with the technology of Egypt—which is to say practically nothing—to build a thing that massive. The cathedrals, the great temples of the world, or the work of any artist who has given his life to producing these things—all of these come from mythic seizure, not from Maslow's values. That awakening of awe, that awakening of zeal, is the beginning, and, curiously enough, that's what pulls people together.

People living for these five values are pushed apart. Two things pull people together: aspiration and terror. These are what glue a society together. Consider the mythological foundation of medieval European society: the great myth of the Fall in the Garden, the redemption on the Cross, and the Church, which was to serve as the sole vessel for the grace of the Redemption and the salvation of mankind. You have an entire society based around the idea that all of us are born tainted with original sin, and that the only way of cleansing this stain from our souls is through the sacraments of the institution of the Church, founded, so it is claimed, by Christ, who is the Incarnation of the God who brought forth the world in the first place. You have this amazing culture whose whole purpose is to cleanse each individual soul from the terrible error of the disobedience in the Garden of Eden.

Saint Paul seems to have been the first one to connect all of these ideas. The entire structure of the medieval community was based on myths of aspiration and terror, and they provide the only way to explain the Middle Ages. There were economic values and the like, but they had nothing to do with the building of Chartres Cathedral. Henry Adams speaks about this in *Mont-Saint-Michel and Chartres*.[47] All of the great cathedrals of Europe were built during this lunatic century between 1150 and 1250. People didn't have enough money then to buy two cows, let alone two cars—what were they living for?

And you mustn't think of slave drivers; that isn't what built the cathedrals. It was a community seizure, a mythic zeal. So what happened? This zeal has disappeared. When doubt came in about the basis of the myth, about the historical truth of Genesis, the whole society fell apart. Aspiration and terror faded, and with them the mythic dream.

I'm sorry to say that things are so infinitely soft for us these days that we're drifting apart. There is no aspiration that's been put in front of us to pull people together, nor any overwhelming fear to drive us together. Well, don't worry about society. What we're focusing on here is pulling yourself together.

How do we find this thing in ourselves, that which truly moves us? Well, as I've said, mythologies are basically the same everywhere. Consequently, mythic images do not refer primarily to historical events. They come from the psyche and talk to the psyche; their primary reference is to the psyche—to the spirit, as we call it—and not to a historical event.

Now, there's no doubt about it that there are certain sensations which spontaneously activate responses in the human body. You don't have to be told what sexual signals are; in fact, very often one isn't told at all, yet the biological imperative takes hold, and everything works just fine. Everything gets started and the parents begin to wonder what's happening. So we don't have to receive instruction there—though it doesn't hurt.

Likewise, certain odors immediately start the salivary glands going. Sleep overtakes you when you find a place to lie down. There are given signals to which the human body responds. These we share with the animals: torpor, activity, sexual zeal, mother love for the just-born creature, aggression toward the one who threatens you, and so on.

There's another level of consciousness in the human psyche, which I would associate with those levels of the wonderful thing that is human consciousness from the heart up to the crown of the head. When the awe and the zeal and the human mind yearning to know are awakened, a new sense of what it is to be human is born. Just as we have a physical body that we share with each other so that we can respond similarly to the same smells, so also we have a spiritual consciousness that is responding to comparable signals, and the whole concept of the archetypes of the human psyche is based on the notion that in the human brain, in the human sympathetic nervous system, there are structures that create a readiness to respond to certain signals. These are shared by all of humanity, with variations individually, but essentially pretty close along the line. And when these are triggered, there is the automatic response, just as there would be to an odor, whether that odor of bananas comes from an African cooking pot or from the fruit basket in my beautiful hotel room. Over the millennia, we have developed some experience of how people respond to spiritual symbols and how contemplating a particular symbol slants the mind places the mind on a certain plane of consciousness, which activates deeper spiritual powers in the individual. Everyone has his own favorites; everyone is ready for an experience unlike that of anybody else. The symbol which you are ready for evokes a response in you.

In our tradition, however, these images—these symbols—have been applied to historical events. In our religious traditions, we interpret the motifs of the Virgin Birth, death, Resurrection, and ascension as particular, temporal episodes. If you begin to doubt the possibility of these occurrences, your faith may be troubled. You will lose the symbol because you reject it. It was given to you as a kind of newspaper report of something that's supposed to have happened somewhere; now, you've studied biology, and you don't even want to consider whether or how a virgin birth can have been accomplished. Is that what it referred to; is that what the mystery is? No, the mystery does not refer to something that might or might not have happened at a certain date in a certain place. It is a motif that is found in myths all over the world, and so must speak to the human psyche in another way entirely.

When these symbols disappear, we have lost the vehicle for communication between our waking consciousness and our deepest spiritual life. We have to reactivate the symbol, to bring it back to life, and to find what it means, to relate it to ourselves in some way or another.

Now, what did Jung do when he decided to seek out his myth? His process of discovery is interesting in that it was so childish. Here he was, thirty-seven years old or so, and he asked himself, What was it I most enjoyed doing as a little boy when I was alone and allowed to play? As it turned out, what he liked to do was put rocks together and make little cities out of stone.

So he said, Why, I'm a big man now, so I'll play with big stones. He bought himself a piece of property in a beautiful place on the lake opposite the city of Zürich. He began planning and building a house in this lovely place, Ascona, and as he worked with his hands, he activated his imagination.

Now, that's the big thing, to activate your imagination somehow. You can't do this by taking suggestions from somebody else. You must find that which your own unconscious wants to meditate on. With his imagination activated, Jung found all kinds of new fantasies coming, dreams of all kinds. He began making records of what he had dreamed and then amplifying it by all kinds of associations.

By doing this, he began the work of discovering his myth. He found that his dreams were becoming very important to him and very rich; he began writing about his dreams in a little journal. He put down each silly little impulse, each theme that came up in his dreams. He recorded the dreams so as to bring them up into his consciousness, and as he kept the journal, the underlying images began coming through. Then he would make pictures of some of these dream things—always in a very solemn way. Now, this book is the kind of thing one would not wish to have published; it is just too private. It was his ceremonial, ritualistic exploration of the place from which the mystery of his life came.

If you keep a dream journal, you'll find the dreams begin piling in on you. You want to go to sleep again and have some more. And you'll find a story is building itself up there. Of course, you have to have a little free time to do this.

Now, my wife, Jean, and I visited Jung and Mrs. Jung at their house at Ascona in 1954. And this was an edifice, all right. It wasn't merely a construction; it was an organic home. It was something that had grown out of the ground. This was a man who was a Swiss from beginning to end. He was born in that beautiful mountain country. He was close to the ground there. His ancestors, particularly on his mother's side, were from the Swiss countryside. His grandfather had come from Germany as a medical man, but Germany, too, in those days was a land-based culture. And he had much of that peasant world in him. Now, for many of us, of course, that wouldn't be the world out of which we've come. We've got to find our own world.

Soon after he began keeping his dream journal, Jung realized that his dreams corresponded to the great mythic themes that he had been studying in working on *Symbols of Transformation*. Mandalas began coming— Jung was the first to become interested in mandalas as a psychological vehicle of self-discovery.

Jung had two good friends who contributed to the development of his insights: Heinrich Zimmer, a great Indologist, who became my own friend and mentor, and Richard Wilhelm, a great Sinologist. These two men had a great knowledge of the mythic lore of India and China, respectively, and they helped Jung to recognize relationships between the symbolic doodles he was putting down from his dreams and Oriental mandalas, the Chinese meditation on the golden flower. With a newly activated imagination, Jung came to the realization that dreams are of two orders: little dreams and big dreams.

Little dreams come from a level of dream consciousness that has to do with quite personal complications. They emerge from the level that has come to be known as the Freudian or unconscious. Little dreams are essentially autobiographical in their character, and there will be nothing in these particular dreams of yours that you would share with others—you are sorting through the expansion of consciousness as it bumps up against the taboos and "thou shalt nots" of your childhood and infancy.

Then comes another kind of dream, where you find yourself facing a problem that's not specific to your peculiar life or social or age situation. Rather, you've run up against one of the great problems of man. These are what Jung called big dreams.

For instance, take the question that I broached a while ago: what is it that supports you in the face of total disaster? At such times, the psyche and the ego consciousness are forced to wrestle with the two huge mysteries of the nature of the cosmos and death. No other animal recognizes itself as being pulled between these two great mysteries. Also, deep within yourself lies the mystery of your own being to be dealt with. Your ego consciousness will be confronted with these overwhelming mysteries—the cosmos, death, and your own depth. When you face these sorts of questions—instead of whether you should or should not go to bed with somebody—you are in a field of profound problems. As it happens, the great mythologies of the world also deal with these problems.

Now, as I've said, these themes are universal. Of course, they occur with different historical inflections here, there, and elsewhere; just so, they'll occur with different inflections in your life from those in anyone else's. For every mythological symbol, there are two aspects to be distinguished: the universal and the local. Adolf Bastian coined the terms *Elementargedanken* and *Völkergedanken* to describe these two aspects.

I find that in India the same two aspects are recognized. There they are called *mārga* and *deśī*, respectively. *Mārga* comes from a root that has to do with an animal trail; it means "the path." By this, Indians mean the path by which the particular aspect of a symbol leads you to personal illumination; it is the path to enlightenment. *Deśī* means "of the province." All mythological symbols, therefore, work in two directions: in the direction of *mārga* and in the direction of *deśī*. The *deśī*, or local, aspect links the individual to the culture.

A mythologically grounded culture presents you with symbols that immediately evoke your participation; they are all vital, living connections, and so they link you both to the underlying mystery and to the culture itself. Yet when that culture uses symbols that are no longer alive, that are no longer effective, it cuts you off. The *mārga* or the *Elementargedanken* provide a path back to the heart of the issue. Looking at the symbol in terms of its universal meaning rather than its local, specific reference takes you down the path to self-discovery and illumination.

The way to find your own myth is to determine those traditional symbols that speak to you and use them, you might say, as bases for meditation. Let them work on you.

A ritual is nothing but the dramatic, visual, active manifestation or representation of a myth. By participating in the rite, you are engaged in the myth, and the myth works on you—provided, of course, that you are caught by the image.

But when you just go through the routine without real commitment, expecting it to work magically and get you into heaven—because you know that when you're baptized, you get into heaven, after all—you've turned away from the proper use of these rites and images.

First, think about your own childhood, as Jung did—the symbols that were put into you then remain. Think not how they relate to an institution, which is probably defunct and likely difficult to respect. Rather, think how the symbols operate on you. Let them play on the imagination, activating it. By bringing your own imagination into play in relation to these symbols, you will be experiencing the *mārga*, the symbols' power to open a path to the heart of mysteries.

It is my belief, drawn from experience, that there's nothing better than comparative mythological studies to let you grasp the big, general form of an image and to give you many different ways of approaching that image. Images are eloquent in themselves; they talk to you. When the intellect tries to explicate an image, one can never exhaust its meaning, one can never exhaust its possibility. Images don't essentially mean anything: they *are*, just as you are. They talk to some kernel in you that *is*.

So ask an artist, "What does your picture mean?" Well, if he despises you enough, he'll tell you.

The point is that if you need him to tell you what it means, then you haven't even seen it. What's the meaning of a sunset? What's the meaning of a flower? What's the meaning of a cow?

The Buddha is called the *tathāgata*, "the one thus come." He is as he is. The universe is "thus come," too. Every piece of it arises out of the same ground. This is called the Doctrine of Mutual Arising.

I had a feeling of this in Japan when I went to Nagasaki, where we dropped the second atom bomb. If the first was a tragedy, the second was an obscenity. There was a great plaza there, immediately below where the bomb had exploded, and there was an enormous statue with a finger pointing up exactly to the point from which the bomb fell. And there was a museum there of everything that had happened to everybody as a result of the bomb. There were murals and pictures, and you could see the whole sweep from that museum of the city that had been wiped out. It has been built up again, a new, modern city, except for this park, which has been preserved as a zone for recollection and reflection.

There I was, an American, the one who had dropped the bomb, and in my relationship with the Japanese, there was no sense of guilt or accusation anywhere, because enemies mutually arise. That which you think happened to you, you brought about. That which you did to others, happened to you. They know this and believe it. This was a real experience, believe me.

All of the dogmatic talk about meanings and moral values and all that has nothing to do with any of that central mystery. It's an *is,* and the way to experience one's own *isness* in relation to the mystery of all mysteries is through handling those elementary mythic images.

Basically, then, there is a level of your dream consciousness that springs from your nature, not from your personal biography. Your nature itself is of two orders. First comes the order of animal nature: the instinct system which is the same in all human beings. Next comes the order of your spiritual life: what goes from the neck up.

No other animal has this great thing up there, this mind. When Dr. Freud began interpreting the inspirations and zeals of the top end of the spinal column in terms of the other end, he misunderstood the whole thing. Since the whole sense of mythological imagery is to propel you up into the spiritual realm, interpreting these things in a purely physical, biological way pulls you down again; it punctures and deflates the symbol. We share with the animals the desire to live, the urge toward survival and security. We share with the animals the zeal for sex and the zeal for winning and prestige—I'm the winner. Yet we bear within us the potential for an entirely different level of experience, a level that can come to us in a moment.

Dante described this enlightened moment in his *Vita nuova*—the moment when he beheld Beatrice, the moment that turned him from a mere human animal into a poet. One might see her as an erotic object, yet what he saw was a manifestation of beauty; he experienced her presence on a different level altogether.

He was struck with what James Joyce called esthetic arrest.[48] That's the beginning of the spiritual life. As Dante tells us in the very first pages of that charming book, "The spirit of my eyes said, 'You behold your delight.' The spirit of life in my heart said, 'You behold your master.' And the spirit of my body said, 'Now you will suffer.'"[49]

Prestige, social relationships, security—all these needs disappeared. She was the end of a beam of mystery that comes from the depth of the universe. When he followed that beam, it led to the very seat of the world's mystery (as it expressed itself in Dante's culture), namely the Trinity.

So, first you must find in yourself that which moves you. Of course, it will move you on the level of a human being. And it should move you in a way appropriate to your stage of life. You must learn to know what the archetype of your stage of life is and live it. Trying to live the archetype of the stage that you have left behind is one of the basic causes of neurotic troubles. I've talked about forty-year-old infants weeping on the Freudian couch. They lack the confidence in their judgments and so forth and are always looking to authorities.

You find this problem, too, when a person tries to hold himself at the apogee. His life has begun to go down, but he thinks he's still up there. So, as we've seen, he goes fishing. Well, a man in his late sixties should be pulling up something better than trout. At least a mermaid or two. And he knows it.

When the mask that you are wearing cracks, when you lose faith in it, you can have a regression into your psyche at any stage of life. When the whole society loses its imagery, it can be in what's called a wasteland situation. This is the situation that we've floundered in for the past century or two. Nothing really means anything because the images of our religion all refer to millennia past, and we're not activating the world in which we live. That's the job of the contemporary poet and artist.

You can find one of the great examples of what happens when a system of social symbols is erased in the North American Indians. Their culture was essentially obliterated during the second half of the nineteenth century. The religious cults and the spiritual life of the hunting communities in the great central plains were based on the relevance of their rites to the buffalo; the buffalo was the central symbol. The animal that was to be killed offered himself as a reigning sacrifice to the human community with the understanding that a certain ritual would be performed to return his blood and life to the soil so that he would live again—we saw this in the Sioux story of the girl who married the buffalo chief. It was a compact of understanding between the animal and human communities, and this was the central ritual matter of the buffalo cult of all of the plains tribes. The whole imagery of the communal psyche was caught up in that ritual cycle.

In the last third of the nineteenth century, the buffalo were slaughtered en masse for two reasons: one, so that they wouldn't be getting in front of the railroad trains that were then going across the continent; but secondly, and perhaps more imperatively, so that the Indians wouldn't have anything to hunt, and they would have to go into the reservations to stay. Bang. The whole social mythology lost its central image. The rites and the songs and the dances—they had no reality anymore. It was all referring back to a time that wasn't there.

And what happened? That was the time when the peyote cult invaded from the Southwest and swept over the plains. You have, too, the ghost dance rituals. The Indians lost their society's outer image, and so they turned inward to find within those forms those supports that had been taken away.

We have the same thing going on in our world right now. When the outer world fails to invoke your psychological participation, you turn inward. You can turn inward with peyote, mescaline, LSD, and all that sort of thing; or you can turn inward with meditations of a different sort.

The best meditation is, of course, to take the religious symbol and not worry about whether it is historically true or not but know that it refers to an interior plane of experience. Choose the images you want to meditate upon. Our world now is what could be called a terminal moraine of broken mythological traditions. All the mythical images of mankind are known to us in the museums and everywhere. And I see among the people questing there—they take an image from Egyptian or the Aztec or almost any culture and use that as a base for a kind of support for their own psyche. What do you think would be better than that?

Now, there's a wonderful work by the poet W. B. Yeats called *A Vision*. Yeats was a relatively older man when he married a young woman named Georgie Hyde-Lees. Very soon after the marriage, she began writing automatically, writing whatever came out of her fingertips without thinking about it. She began writing the whole philosophy of Yeats—which he didn't even know about yet. Now that's the kind of girl to marry.

What she wrote—what came out of her—was a very mysterious thing. Yeats received this information as a revelation from spirit informants—he was something of an occultist. *A Vision* is very complicated, but there is one system of images there that seems to me very important for our present concern. It pertains to what he calls the masks, the mask that you've got to put on in order to live. Obviously, this philosophy ties in with Jung's idea of the persona. You have to put a mask on; you have to wear a costume; you have to be something, or seem to be something, at any rate. But there's more to it.

In the book, Yeats speaks of what he calls the primary mask, which is the role that society expects you to play. When you are born, your parents begin communicating to you patterns of life that define the society that each particular parent happens to care for. The hope is that the childhood teachings will lead you into life. The first half of life is about engagement in the world. Here you find the *deśī:* the imagery of local culture, attracting you to the world so that you choose to enter into it. Society and your parents encourage you to make an effort to live in accordance with the possibilities that the society recognizes in you.

When I was a little kid, we used to play a game with buttons: "Rich man, poor man, beggar man, thief."

"Well, what are you going to be?"

"I'm going to be a garbageman." That's a great prospect—the primary mask that you take from society.

There is a second kind of mask that Yeats and his wife call the antithetical mask. And so, it begins to get exciting. Just at the age of middle adolescence, when you come to maturity, there begins to dawn on you the prospect of your own life, which is not the same as that which society has put upon you. "They never saw me before! I am a unique thing. There are great things in me, and, by gosh, I'm going to find out what they are!" And so you discover the problem of finding your own myth.

Mr. and Mrs. Yeats work out this conflict between the primary and antithetical masks through the image of the twenty-eight days of the month. On the first day of the cycle, it's dark—you are born. You begin to grow, mostly in darkness. Nature and society urge you to move on, bearing the primary mask.

At the end of the first week—the eighth day of the moon—comes the phase of the half-moon, the time of adolescence and, more importantly, the awakening of the potential of the full moon, namely the antithetical mask. Suddenly, you burn to find your own zeal, to find your own destiny, and to live it. There comes a sense of great tension with the primary mask and the society that put it upon you. You experience a desire to break away, to break through: "let me be." One fights through, with good fortune or bad.

On the fifteenth day of the cycle, we get the full moon. On this day, the antithetical mask reaches fulfillment: midcareer, midlife. If you're going to be anything, it's what you are at that moment.

Then the darkness begins to come down again. By the twenty-second day, the primary mask is taking over again; nature has moved back in. The remains of your individual life become smaller and smaller and smaller, and you're spending most of your time tending to doctors and sleep and all of that kind of business.

Finally, of course, on the twenty-eighth day—extinction.

This is the mystery of life and its masks. What're you going to do when the thing breaks, and it starts winding down? Are you just going to become an old dog getting older and older, sinking back into your body? Or in the moment of the full moon have you made the jump to the solar light?

On the Great Plains in the center of America, one may have this experience once every month. On the fifteenth day of each lunar cycle, the sun sets in the west just as the full moon rises in the east. They're exactly the same size, even the same color, and they're visible at exactly the same moment. That's the moment of the fullness of your powers in midlife, when your zeal for your own life has reached its apogee. From that moment it must remain in your spirit, in your mind. The moon is symbolic of the body's life, which carries its death within it. The sun is symbolic of the pure spirit that has no darkness, no death in it. It is this pure spirit that can watch with compassion as your body goes the way of all bodies. It can share in the amplitude of your spiritual experience of the life of all creatures.

I'll often tell a group in a lecture hall to look up at the source of illumination in the room. Now, we can speak of this illumination as light or as several lights. Each of these ways of looking provides a general principle, namely light.

Now, when a bulb breaks, nobody's going to say, "Oh, dear, we did love that bulb, and this is a great, great shame." If you do love it particularly—if it has a certain shape or something like that—you can take it out and put it on the bureau, but you're not going to be too greatly concerned; you put another bulb in.

You can think of the world in two ways: one, in the way of separate bulbs, and the other, in the way of a general light that shows itself through bulbs. Now, if I look down at the people in the hall, I don't see bulbs, I see heads. What's in the heads? Consciousness. Each head is a vehicle of consciousness. Now, with what do you identify yourself? Is it with the bulb or is it with the light? Is it with the body or is it with the consciousness? I'm speaking now of basic mythological motifs. The concern of youth is to bring this vehicle—one's body—to fulfillment at maturity in such a way that it will be the best possible carrier of consciousness. And at that moment, one shifts the center of gravity from concern for the vehicle of consciousness to identity with consciousness itself. When you have identified your life with consciousness, you will find the body can go. That is the great crisis at the full moon.

It is just the crisis that Dante says he experienced in his thirty-fifth year; this is the vision of *The Divine Comedy,* in which the whole universe becomes a manifestation not so much of consciousness, in his vocabulary, as of love. He identified himself with that love, that grace which proceeds from the transcendent throne and shows itself in the beautiful vehicles of which Beatrice was one.

No culture except the modern and late-medieval European culture has allowed individuals to develop the antithetical mask. In the Western world, our mythologies typically intend to awaken Yeats's antithetical mask. It's a wonderful word for it, because it is antithetical in a certain sense, antithetical to the primary mask. That antithetical mask, like the unconscious self in Jung's model of the unconscious, represents the potential of your fulfillment.

All Oriental cultures require that you live according to the patterns that the culture puts upon you. In other words, they expect you to identify with the primary mask, with what Freud called the superego. In India, they call it dharma, or duty; in China, it is called the Tao, the path or way. In either case, the concept means identifying yourself with the culture image.

So, to follow the argument to its end, you do not have what Westerners might call human beings in such a culture; you have repetitions of what there was before. You have a society of beings being just what the culture says that beings ought to be. They die, and there's another generation doing exactly the same things: the fully realized static society. The character of Occidental culture, rather, pushes us to identify with the antithetical mask.

We keep hearing about the revolution around us all the time: the revolution, the revolution, the revolution. Revolution doesn't have to do with smashing something; it has to do with bringing something forth. If you spend all your time thinking about that which you are attacking, then you are negatively bound to it. You have to find the zeal in yourself and bring that out. That is what's given to you—one life to live. Marx teaches us to blame the society for our frailties; Freud teaches us to blame our parents for our frailties; astrology teaches us to blame the universe. The only place to look for blame is within: you didn't have the guts to bring up your full moon and live the life that was your potential.

The Functions of Mythology in Tradition and Today

Let me very briefly touch once again on the functions that a traditional mythology presents. I'd like to look at how much of this traditional mythology (and its functions) remains in our lives today.

The first function is awakening in the individual a sense of awe and mystery and gratitude for the ultimate mystery of being. In the old traditions—the very old ones—the accent was on saying yea to the world as it is. That's not easy; you look at the world, and you see creatures eating each other, killing each other, and you realize that life is something that eats itself.

You may have the feeling that some have had, that this cannibalism is just too horrible to bear: "I will not cooperate, I will not play." This change in thinking I call the Great Reversal. Historically, it comes along about the sixth century B.C. with the Buddha's statement "All life is sorrowful." Well, there is escape from sorrow.

"I won't play."

"Okay. Pull out. Take your bat and ball and go home."

So here we have two main attitudes toward the central horrific mystery, this thing beyond good and evil: affirmation and negation.

Zoroastrianism introduced a third way of reacting to life's terrible mystery in the idea of two deities, one good and one evil. One god represented truth and light, and the other represented darkness and lies. The good deity created a good world, and the evil deity corrupted that world. So the world that we're in is a corrupt world. There is a contest going on between the powers of light and the powers of darkness, and you are invited to join the forces of the light against the forces of darkness and struggle to reconstitute the good world. Neither affirming nor negating life as is, this—one might call it compromise—presents a sort of progressive view.

As far as I've been able to discover, these are the three views of life as life. You can live in total affirmation. As one of the Buddhist aphorisms states marvelously: "This world—just as it is with all its horror, all its darkness, all its brutality—is the golden lotus world of perfection." If you don't see it as such, that's not the world's fault. You can't improve what is perfect. You can only see it and so come to realize your own perfection. That is to say, you can come to that depth in yourself which is deeper than the pains and sorrows. You have deities named *bhairavānanda:* "the bliss and ecstasy of terror."[50] That's what life is—a terrible, terrible ordeal.

The life-negating way seeks purity: "I am so spiritual, I will go through the sun door and not participate in this darkness of the lunar cycle at all, and you won't see me coming back."

The progressive or ameliorative way says, "Let's get in there and improve it." This is like marrying someone in order to improve that person. I don't call this affirmation. It usually puts you in the position of being a little bit superior: "If God had only asked me, I could have given Him some pointers."

Now, the second function serves to present a universe within which the mystery as understood will be present, so that everywhere you look it is, as it were, a holy picture, opening up in back to the great mystery.

The work of the artist is to present objects to you in such a way that they will shine. Through the rhythm of the artist's formation, the object that you have looked at with indifference will be radiant, and you will be fixed in esthetic arrest.

In our cosmology today, we envision a prodigious universe that isn't matched at all by the little kindergarten thing presented by our religious tradition. Think of the moon walk. To me, man's first walk on the moon is the most important mythological event of the twentieth century. Before everybody's eyes, that one event transformed the fundamental basis for our view of the universe and ourselves within that universe. In all earlier periods, the notion was that these lights—the moon, Mercury, Mars, Venus, and all the rest—represented the radiance of a higher mode of being, much higher than this poor miserable earth. When Galileo recognized that the laws of ballistics on earth are the laws that operate on the planets, he began something that reached fulfillment in these strolls on the lunar surface.

I remember hearing a great, cosmologically profound statement from the trip before the first moon walk, *Apollo 10*. When they had circled the moon and were coming back—just after they had read the first verses of Genesis—the astronauts were asked who was navigating. They answered, "Newton."

In his introduction to *Metaphysics,* Kant asked the question, "How is it that I can make mathematical calculations in this space here that I know, with apodictic certainty, will be valid in that space over there?"[51] How is it that I can be so sure of the continuity of space that I know that the laws which my head can evolve will be valid elsewhere? When it came to going down onto the moon, nobody knew how deep the dust was going to be. I'll never forget that first foot coming down; it was a terrific moment—man on the moon. Nobody knew what it was going to be like, yet they did know just how many ounces of fuel to emit from those jets to bring that craft back within a mile of the boat that was waiting for it in the Pacific Ocean.

In other words, the laws of space and mass and energy were precisely known to man; we carry those laws within our own heads. The laws of time and space and causality are in us, and anything we can see or know anywhere will involve these laws. What is the universe? Space. Out of space came a coagulation that became a nebula, and out of the nebula, millions of galaxies, and within one constellation of galaxies, a sun, with our little planet circling it. Then out of the earth came us, the eyes and the consciousness and the ears and the breathing of the earth itself. We're earth's children, and, since the earth itself came out of space, is it any wonder that the laws of space live in us? There's this wonderful accord between the exterior and interior worlds, and it's not as though God had breathed anything into us; the gods we know are projections of our own fantasies, our own consciousness, our own deep being. They are our match, in a way.

Well, when I state it that way, you can see that ours is simply another mythology, expressed in another cosmology. Every time you look at the moon now, think about it that way, and you'll have a very different experience.

The third, sociological function of mythology gives you laws for living within your own society. Of course, no society today is in a position to say that it knows what the laws for the next ten years are going to be. Everything that we thought was good has turned out to be inconvenience. We have this whole ecological crisis, and all this kind of business. Every day drives home the fact that the laws of life have to change along with the modes of life. So we don't have security. We have to wing it.

The final, pedagogical function of mythology gives the individual a way to connect the inner psychological world to the external world of phenomena. As I've tried to suggest, the pedagogy of our inherited traditions does not work for all of us, so you have to work out your own pedagogy. Now, let me give a notion of the ways, as Jung describes them, in which the mythic images come to life in you.

I had a very amusing experience once lecturing in the Pacific Northwest. I was talking about Dante's view of the ages of man—he, too, came up with an astrological schema for the great cycle of life.

Unlike the Yeatses with their lunar metaphor, Dante likens life to the daily transit of the sun. He names four ages, each of which corresponds to a time of day, and each of which has its proper set of virtues. The first is infancy, which goes to the age of twenty-five, would you believe. The qualities for infancy are obedience, a sense of shame, comeliness of appearance, and sweetness of conduct. This is the morning.

Then you come, at the age of twenty-five, to what he calls maturity, and this stage will last to year forty-five. You have reached the high moment of life, and for this stage he names the values of the medieval knight: temperance, courage, love, courtesy, and loyalty. When you have lived your life in terms of what the society asks of you, you will come to a moment at midcareer, at around thirty-five, when you will actually have the experience of what, formerly, you had simply been taught; then you are eligible to teach. This is the afternoon.

Dante calls the age from forty-five to seventy the age of wisdom. In India, the wise get sent out to the forest; not here in the West. Here we expect the aged to stay in society, look around with a critical eye, and share the benefit of their experience. At this stage, the qualities are wisdom, justice, generosity, and humor or cheerfulness. After all, you've got nothing to lose; you've reached the evening.

From seventy on he calls decrepitude, and the qualities are looking back over your life with gratitude and forward to death as a return home. Now it is night.

This little schedule, this life pattern—this is mythos.

In any case, when I'd finished my lecture up in Seattle, one young lady came up to me, and she said, very seriously, "Oh, Mr. Campbell, you just don't know about the modern generation. We go directly from infancy to wisdom."

I said, "That is great. All you've missed is life."

So, I say the way to find your myth is to find your zeal, to find your support, and to know what stage of life you're in. The problems of youth are not the problems of age. Don't try to live your life too soon. By listening too much to gurus, you try to jump over the whole darn thing and back off and become wise before you've experienced that in relation to which there is some point to being wise. This thing, wisdom, has to come gradually.

There are something like 18 billion cells in the brain alone. There are no two brains alike; there are no two hands alike; there are no two human beings alike. You can take your instructions and your guidance from others, but you must find your own path, just like one of Arthur's knights seeking the Grail in the forest.

It is this quality of the Occidental spirit that strikes other cultures as so silly and romantic. What is it we are questing for? It is the fulfillment of that which is potential in each of us. Questing for it is not an ego trip; it is an adventure to bring into fulfillment your gift to the world, which is yourself.

There's nothing you can do that's more important than being fulfilled. You become a sign, you become a signal, transparent to transcendence; in this way, you will find, live, and become a realization of your own personal myth.

CHAPTER VI

THE SELF AS HERO[52]

In the West, you have the liberty and the obligation of finding out what your destiny is.[53] You can discover it for yourself. But do you?

Of course, it doesn't hurt to be blessed with the accident of money, and a certain amount of support, and a margin of free time. But let me say this: people without money very often have the courage to risk a life of their own, and they can do it. Money doesn't count, it's not that important in our culture; it really isn't.

I've taught students of all financial strata, and the most fortunate are not always the very wealthy ones. In fact, they're very often the least fortunate because there's nothing to drive them. A very common experience is a student who has all kinds of possibilities and talents and essentially limitless money and becomes nothing more than a dilettante. The student is not forced to follow one path, to make a decision: "I'm going to do this." As soon as what they are doing gets difficult, as soon as it begins to get to the crunch, he or she moves over into another pursuit, and another, and another. They just splash their lives all over. Very often a youngster without the margin to do that makes the intelligent, courageous decision and follows it through.

Now, I'm not saying that we are perfect on that point here in the

United States, or in the West. Yet the opportunity is there for each person with the courage to seek a destiny. There are several ways of discovering your destiny.

The first is in retrospect. In a wonderful essay called "On an Apparent Intention in the Fate of the Individual," Schopenhauer points out that, once you have reached an advanced age, as I have, as you look back over your life, it can seem to have had a plot, as though composed by a novelist.[54] Events that seemed entirely accidental or incidental turn out to have been central in the composition.

So who composed that plot? Schopenhauer's idea is that, just like our dreams, our lives are directed by what he called the will, that self of which we are largely unconscious. We have been, he says, dreamers of our own lives, like Viṣṇu on his seven-headed serpent.

I brought out my book *Myths to Live By* by collecting together a series of lectures that I had given at Cooper Union over a period of twenty-four years.[55] My notion about myself was that I had grown up during that time, that my ideas had changed, and, too, that I had progressed. But when I brought these papers together, they were all saying essentially the same thing—over a span of decades. I found out something about the thing that was moving me. I didn't even have a very clear idea of what it was until I recognized those continuities running through that whole book. Twenty-four years is a pretty good stretch of time; a lot had happened during that period. And there I was babbling on about the same thing. That's my myth in there.

Another astonishing way to look back is to pick up some diary entries or notes that you kept a long time ago. You'll be astonished. Things that you were convinced you had realized more recently will be all pinned down there. These are driving themes in your life.

But what if you want to gain some idea of what your myth is while you are living it? Well, another way to try to discern your destiny—your myth—would be to follow Jung's example: observe your dreams, observe your conscious choices, keep a journal, and see which images and stories surface and resurface. Look at stories and symbols and see which ones resonate.

I would like now to review the archetypal myth of the hero's journey as I dealt with it in *The Hero with a Thousand Faces*.[56] This is what Joyce called the monomyth: an archetypal story that springs from the collective unconscious. Its motifs can appear not only in myth and literature, but, if you are sensitive to it, in the working out of the plot of your own life.

The basic story of the hero journey involves giving up where you are, going into the realm of adventure, coming to some kind of symbolically rendered realization, and then returning to the field of normal life.

The first stage is leaving where you are, whatever the environment. You may leave because the environment is too repressive and you are consciously uneasy and eager to leave. Or it may be that a *call to adventure,* an alluring temptation, comes and draws you out. In European myths this call is frequently represented by some animal—a stag or boar—that manages to elude a hunter and brings him into a part of the forest that he doesn't recognize. And he doesn't know where he is, how to get out, or where he should go. And then the adventure begins.

Another obvious case of the call to adventure occurs when something—or someone—has been taken away and you then go in quest of it into the realms of adventure. Always, the realm of adventure is one of unknown forces and unknown powers.

On the other hand, there may come what I call a refusal of the call, where the summons is heard or felt, and perhaps even heeded, but for one reason or another cut off. One thinks of some reason for not going, or one has fear or something like this and one remains; the results are then radically different from those of the one following the call.

I think the shaman's crisis is the most vivid and interesting example of the call in real life. In researching the first volume of my *Historical Atlas of World Mythology,*[57] I came across many examples of this, from tribes around the world. Typically the young person is walking alone on the ocean shore or in the mountains or in the forest, and hears an unearthly music; this music then is accompanied by some kind of visionary visitation, which amounts to a summons.

Now, being a shaman is no fun in any of these societies, and a lot of young people just don't want to accept it. Unfortunately, those who choose to refuse the call don't have a life. Either they die, or, in trying to lead more mundane lives, they exist as nonentities, what T. S. Eliot called "hollow men."[58]

Earlier, I mentioned the case of the West Virginia woman who was in analysis late in her life. She was overwhelmed by the feeling that she had missed her life, that she was just a shell. Through analysis, fishing back, she remembered wandering in the woods and hearing wonderful music; unfortunately, she hadn't known what to do about this experience. And ever since then, she had not been living the life that this music had called her to. If she had been in a primitive community, her family and the tribal shaman would have known just what to do. When the call isn't answered, you experience a kind of drying up and a sense of life lost.

If the call is heeded, however, the individual is invoked to engage in a dangerous adventure. It's always a dangerous adventure because you're moving out of the familiar sphere of your community. In myths, this is represented as moving out of the known sphere altogether into the great beyond. I call this crossing the threshold. This is the crossing from the conscious into the unconscious world, but the unconscious world is represented in many, many, many different images, depending on the cultural surroundings of the mythos. It may be a plunge into the ocean, it may be a passage into the desert, it may be a getting lost in a dark forest, it may be finding yourself in a strange city. It may be depicted as an ascent or as a descent or as a going beyond the horizon, but this is the adventure—it's always the path into the unknown, through the gateway or the cave or the clashing rocks.

One asks: what is the meaning of this business of the clashing rocks? It's a wonderful image. We live, on this side of the mystery, in the realm of the pairs of opposites: true and false, light and dark, good and evil, male and female, and all that dualistic rational worldview. One can have an intuition that is beyond good and evil, that goes beyond pairs of opposites—that's the opening of this gateway into the mystery. But it's just one of those little intuitive flashes, because the conscious mind comes back again and closes the door. The idea in the hero adventure is to walk bodily through the door into the world where the dualistic rules don't apply.

Now, when I was in India, I wanted to meet a real, first-class master. And I didn't want to hear any more slop about *māyā* and having to give up the world and all that kind of stuff. I'd had enough of that for fifteen or twenty years. I was checking around, and I heard of one master in Trivandrum, a lovely little city down in southwest India. His name was Sri Krishna Menon.[59]

Through quite a series of adventures, I managed to get an audience with this wonderful little man. He was seated in one chair and I was in the other—this was quite a confrontation. Of course, the first thing he says is, "Do you have a question?"

I had the good fortune, I learned later, to ask exactly the question that had been *his* first question to his guru. The question I asked was this: "Since all is *brahman*, since all is the divine radiance, how can we say no to anything? How can we say no to ignorance? How can we say no to brutality? How can we say no to anything?"

To this he said, "For you and me, we say yes." Then he gave me a little meditation—and it's a good one: where are you between two thoughts? You're thinking of yourself all the time, everything you do. You know, there's the image of yourself—your ego. So, where are you between two thoughts?

That's what that intuitive flash is giving you a taste of. This thought, that thought, the ripple of the mind—do you ever have a glimpse that transcends anything you could think of about yourself? That's the source field out of which all of your energies are coming. And so the hero journey through the threshold is simply a journey beyond the pairs of opposites, where you go beyond good and evil. That is the sense of the image of the clashing rocks, there's simply no doubt about it.

This motif is known also, mythologically, as the active door. This mythic device appears in American Indian stories, in Greek stories, in Eskimo stories, in stories from all over. It is an archetypal image that communicates the sense of going past judgment.

Another challenge at the threshold can be the encounter with the dark counterpart, the shadow, where the shining hero meets the dark. It may be in the form of a dragon, or it may be in the form of a malignant enemy. In either case, the hero has to slay the other and go into the other world alive.

On the other hand, another image for this passage is dismemberment, where the hero is chopped into pieces. In this case, you enter the realm of adventure dead. You get this in the story of the Egyptian god Osiris, where he's killed, dismembered, and then put together again. This is a typical event in this kind of story; think of the father of the buffalo bride in the Blackfoot story, who is stomped to bits and then resurrected.

In this sort of story, after the trial has been passed, you have a resurrection from death. There are many, many ways of representing this journey and many ways of experiencing it. Sometimes it is personified—a confrontation with demons or gods, as in the *Tibetan Book of the Dead*—while other times in myths and dreams it appears more like the journey across a dark ocean or through a mountain.

In any case, whether chopped up, nailed to a cross, or swallowed by a whale, you are passing into the realm of death. Christ on the Cross is making that passage: the Cross is the threshold to the adventure of his reunion with God the Father.

Once you have crossed the threshold, if it really is your adventure—if it is a journey that is appropriate to your deep spiritual need or readiness—helpers will come along the way to provide magical aid. This may be some little wood sprite or wise man or fairy godmother or animal that comes to you as a companion or as an adviser, letting you know what the dangers are along the way and how to overcome them. You are given little tokens that will protect you, images to meditate on, *mudrās*—gestures or postures of the hand—and mantras—words to chant and think on—that will guide you and keep you on the path. It's a narrow path, the sword bridge, and if you fall off that, you are in a helpless condition because you don't know what to do and there's nobody around to help you.

After you have received the magical aid, you will have a series of increasingly threatening tests or trials to pass. The deeper you get into this gauntlet, the heavier the resistance. You are coming into areas of the unconscious that have been repressed: the shadow, the anima/animus, and the rest of the unintegrated self; it is that repression system that you have to pass through. This, of course, is where the magical aid is most required.

These tests, then, symbolize self-realization, a process of initiation into the mysteries of life. There are four kinds of hurdles along this road of trials that I think represent all of the possibilities.

The first is the symbol of the erotic encounter with the perfect beloved; I call this meeting the goddess. This is the challenge of integrating the anima/animus. In the mythic vocabulary of alchemy, this is called the sacred marriage, or *hieros gamos.* Jung writes about the symbolism of this union a good deal.[60] In myths of the man's adventure, the sacred marriage is union with the world goddess or with some minor secondary representation of her power. This is the story of the prince reaching Sleeping Beauty, of Rāma's marriage to Sītā in the *Rāmāyaṇa.*

If you are unready, however, the goddess may appear in a less-benign form. Actaeon, who is utterly out of touch with his anima, comes across Artemis naked in the pool and is destroyed by the encounter. She turns him into a stag, and he is hunted to death by his own hounds. She can also appear as a temptress, a succubus leading you astray from your true path.

In the woman's case, this divine union is frequently represented by being fecundated by a god. Ovid's *Metamorphoses* is full of gods pursuing nymphs; the god appears as a bull or a golden shower, and suddenly you've got a little bundle of joy. The child then becomes symbolic of the coordination of the opposites, male and female. Of course, this is the real meaning of the motif of the Virgin Birth. It represents the woman receiving inspiration for the new life through a divine visitation.

In myths of this kind, the next stage of the adventure, of course, is bearing the child and, frequently, fostering it, as Jochebed gives up Moses. Remember, however, that the child here does not represent a physical child; it is spiritual life.

So, the first stage along the road is the sacred marriage. The fairy tale always ends in that kind of thing: the couple kiss and live happily ever after. Well, as someone who has been happily married for almost half a century, I can say with authority that *happily ever after* is just the beginning. Like life, most myths go on from there.

The second kind of fulfillment along the road of trials is what is called atonement with the father, and this trial is definitely a male rite of passage. The son has been separated from the father; he has been living a life inappropriate to his true heritage. Perhaps he has been living like a girl, as Achilles does, or a farm boy, as Parsifal does. Perhaps he has been taken in as a prince, but for the wrong people, as happens to Moses. As he struggles along his quest, he finds the father, who is really in the abyss beyond the mother—you might say he has to go through the mother's world to reach the father's.

In stories of atonement with the father, the woman becomes either the guide or the seductress that blocks the way. Now, in Indian thought, *māyā*, the feminine principle that engenders the phenomenal universe, has both a revealing power and an obscuring power. In her obscuring guise, she becomes the witch, and in her revealing form, she is the guiding woman clothed in light, the Lady of the Lake.

In Christian symbology, the father atonement is the primary image; Christ goes straight through the Cross to the Father. Frequently, in images of the Crucifixion, you have Mary standing at the foot of the Cross. Now, in many cultures, the cross is the sign of both the earth and of the feminine principle. Mary is the cross; she was Christ's gateway from eternity to the field of time, and now she is the gateway back. Birth into the world is the crucifixion of the spirit, and the crucifixion of the body releases the spirit back into eternity.

In George Lucas's film *The Return of the Jedi,* Luke Skywalker risks his life to redeem the life of his father, Darth Vader—this is the father-atonement motif played out on a grand scale: the son saves the father and the father saves the son.

The third station along the path to fulfillment is apotheosis, where you realize that you are what you are seeking. The ultimate example of this is when Gautama Śākyamuni achieves Buddhahood and realizes, "I am the Buddha."

These are the three main realization symbols: the *hieros gamos,* the reconciliation with the animus and anima; the atonement with the father; and apotheosis, coming to realize the full scope of yourself, like Guatama seated under the bo tree becoming the knower of himself as an incarnation of the universal Buddha consciousness.

The fourth kind of realization is of a quite different spirit. Instead of a slow progress through the mysteries, there is a violent rush through all obstacles and the seizing of the desired boon: the Promethean theft of fire. A variation on this theme is the bride quest—the hero has lost his beloved and goes to steal her back from the ogre who has taken her. Rāma's wife Sītā is abducted by Rāvana, the demon king. Much of the *Rāmāyaṇa* concerns Rāma's recovery of Sītā—that's the bride quest.

In any case, once the treasure has been grabbed, there is no reconciliation with the powers of the underworld—no sacred marriage, father atonement, nor apotheosis—so there is a violent reaction of the whole unconscious system against the act, and the hero must escape.

This is a psychotic condition. You have wrenched some knowledge from the deepest abysses of your unknown self, and now the demons have been loosed to wreak their vengeance.

Now you find the wonderful motif known as the magic flight, which is quite a favorite in fairy tales and American Indian stories. The fleeing hero keeps throwing over his or her shoulder combs that turn into forests and pebbles that turn into mountains and mirrors that turn into lakes, and so on. A monster is in mad pursuit—it's usually an ogress following, as the unconscious frequently comes up in the guise of the mother power in its violent, negative aspect.

There comes the crossing of the line again, what I call the return across the threshold. The line through which you passed when you went into the abyss is the line through which you pass when you leave the powers behind. But can you get back up into the world of light? Is there going to be spontaneous remission, you might say, or are you going to remain the prey of these powers underneath?

Now, the crises of descent and return will match. If you make the descent by being swallowed by a whale, for instance—as Jonah is, being swallowed by the abyss—at the end you'll be thrown back up out of the whale. If you passed into the adventure through water—Joseph in the well or Odysseus on the wine-dark sea—you'll return through the water: Moses leading the hero of the Old Testament, the People, through the Red Sea or Odysseus washed up on the shores of Ithaca. If you enter the path of adventure by passing through the Symplegades, the clashing rocks, then you come back out through something of that kind as well.

The whole idea is that you've got to bring out again that which you went to recover, the unrealized, unutilized potential in yourself. The whole point of this journey is the reintroduction of this potential into the world; that is to say, to you living in the world. You are to bring this treasure of understanding back and integrate it in a rational life. It goes without saying, this is very difficult. Bringing the boon back can be even more difficult than going down into your own depths in the first place.

Let's say a young man comes to New York to study art. He's gone from Wisconsin into the underworld, Greenwich Village, and there he finds all of these nymphs who tempt and inspire him, and there's a master there with whom he's studying, and so forth, and finally, through their assistance and through his own hard work and talent, he achieves his own art style.

The first crisis is that he must not have the art style of the master but find his own style. That's a very important moment in any creative studio. I've seen very funny things. Sometimes you have a master who doesn't want his students to have any other style, you know, and then the student, when his own spirit begins to take over, has this violent hatred of the person who has been the master.

Finally, having achieved his individual style, he comes to 57th Street to sell his paintings, and he meets the cold eye of the dealer. The point is that what you have to bring is something that the world lacks—that is why you went to get it. Well, the daylight world doesn't even know that it needs this gift you are bringing. There are three possible reactions, then, when you come to the return threshold, carrying your boon for the world.

The first is that there is no reception at all. No one cares about this great treasure you have brought. What are you going to do? One answer is to say to yourself, "To hell with them. I'm going back to Wisconsin." And then you buy yourself a dog and a pipe and let the weeds grow in the gate, and you're painting pictures that will be discovered two thousand years from now and recognized as the greatest paintings of the twentieth century. You go back into your own newly unified whole and let the world go stink.

The second way is to say, "What do they want?" Now you've got a skill, and you can give 'em what they're asking for. This is what's known as commercial art. You keep saying to yourself, "When I get enough money, I'm going to stop and do my big thing." Of course, it never happens, because you've created a whole pitch for your expression that doesn't allow you to get out what you had before; it gets lost. But you have a public career, which is something.

The third possibility is to try to find some aspect of, or some portion of, the domain into which you have come that can receive some little portion of what you have to give. This is the pedagogical attitude of helping them to realize the need, what you needed and have got to give. Those are the only possibilities.

The first is the refusal of the return, you see. The second is the return in terms of the society, so you're not giving them a goddamn thing: they're only getting what they want. And the third is a pedagogical attitude of trying to find a means or a vocabulary or something that will enable you to deliver to them what you have found as the life boon in terms, and in proportions, that are proper to their ability to receive. You can always do this, but this requires a good deal of compassion and patience.

If nothing else, you can get a job teaching.

But you will find, if you make one little hook into the society, that you presently will be able to deliver your message. I know it.

An artist who has discovered his own style, his own voice, comes back and takes a teaching job, teaching art. Perhaps that's not giving all that he has, but it's giving something that he has that is in line with what he has to give and what the society is ready to receive. He's receiving an adequate income to sustain him while he goes on with his painting here and gradually builds up a gallery public.

For myself, I was out in the woods in the middle of the Depression with nothing to do but read, and I read for five years without a job. You see, in my youth, in the days of the Depression, people who were what might be called counterculture had been kicked out of the society entirely. There was no room for them. That's different from the ones who leave out of resentment or with the intention to improve it.

What did I do? I read. I followed the path from one book to another, from one thinker to another. I followed my bliss, though I didn't know that that was what I was doing.

Then I got a job. I'd been immersed in Spengler and Jung and Schopenhauer and Joyce, and finally this little message comes: would you like a job teaching literature at Sarah Lawrence? Well, when I saw those girls, I knew I wanted the job. And the salary was $2,200 for the year.

I was willing to get back into the world and share what I had learned. I had been following a star; I really found everything that I am sharing here during those five years.

Just around the time that I started teaching, this amazing book came out: *Finnegans Wake*. And no one understood it—no one but me and a couple of other crazy Irishmen. Everything that Joyce was writing about came straight out of what I'd been immersing myself in during those five years in the wilderness. Well, I turned to one of the other crazies, my colleague Henry Morton Robinson, and I said, "Some fools have got to explain this to everyone. They might as well be you and I." And that was my first book, *A Skeleton Key to Finnegans Wake*.[61]

Even at that, we worked for five years on that thing and couldn't sell it. We were just at the point of thinking, Well, we'll publish it ourselves—which would have cost a hell of a lot of money—when I went to see Thornton Wilder's *The Skin of Our Teeth,* which was the big Broadway hit at the time. And all I heard was *Finnegans Wake.* I was the only person in the city that knew this. I was catching these quotations as they were coming down. Well, this is the way you get back into the world.

I phoned Robinson, and I said, "Good God, here's Wilder making tons of money and a lot of fame on this thing, and it's simply *Finnegans Wake.*"

Joyce had just died, and his family was destitute. So I said, "I think we should write a letter to the *New York Times.*" I went up and just told him what I had heard because the play hadn't been published yet.

So he phones down to Norman Cousins at the *Saturday Review* and says, "*Skin of Our Teeth* is *Finnegans Wake,* are you interested?"

Cousins says, "Bring it down this evening."

So we float this little article to Cousins. He reads it over, and the first thing he says is, "Let's call it 'The Skin of Whose Teeth?'" He publishes it, and we got headlines all over the United States.[62]

Then every columnist in the country comes pouncing into us like a bunch of dive-bombers. We're in the war now, do you see? And Wilder's now Captain Wilder, then Major Wilder, practically General Wilder. Well, who's this pair of Irishmen? And that Mick over there, Joyce, with his *Ulysses* and his *Finnegans*—this is not a civilization we're fighting for. And it wasn't. But nobody could read *Finnegans Wake,* so they didn't know whether we had told the truth or not.

So they went to Wilder, and that son of a gun, when they would ask him about our article, he would say, "Well, watch my play and read *Finnegans Wake* and see what you think." Of course, they couldn't read it.

The pretense was that he was the great American artist and this was folk stuff that he had brought up right out of the American soil. He said the whole thing occurred to him at a silly musical called *Hellzapoppin;* his play landed in his lap like Athena newborn from Zeus's brow.

Well, this was all bilge. I said to Robinson, "Cool it, just wait. Let this one shout."

Presently out comes *Skin of Our Teeth* in book form. It's up for the Pulitzer and the Tony. Well, I went through that script with a fine-tooth comb and found nearly two hundred and fifty analogues—characters, themes, and finally a four-line, word-for-word quote.

So out comes "The Skin of Whose Teeth? Part II." We laid out the parallels side by side. And that was that. He didn't get the critics' award.

So Cousins says, "Do you two guys have anything else?" So we thought, Let's give him the first chapter of *A Skeleton Key.* And he passed it along to Harcourt Brace, which had already refused the book once. They sent that chapter over to T. S. Eliot, who wrote back, "Buy it."

That's how we sold it. Now that's how you get back into the world. There was a lot of work, but there has to be luck.

There's another possibility. I knew an artist up in Woodstock, where I spent most of the Depression. He had a good public, with a gallery, and he had a fairly typical commercial style. One year, he had a transformation. He went through a psychological breakthrough, and he developed a much more brilliant, daring way of handling the brush. He brings this to his gallery, and they say, "We don't want it. Your public wants pictures like the ones you've been doing all along."

Success can become a kind of trap. This is really true in the United States—I don't think it's quite that way elsewhere. There was a typical pattern to all of the novelists that had been published in the twenties—Sinclair Lewis, Theodore Dreiser, Ernest Hemingway, F. Scott Fitzgerald, and the rest. They would write an early work, one that showed talent, and then another work that was further advanced in handling the form, and then another one—and that's the one that suddenly catches the public's attention. Then they try to hold on to that and their writing goes down and down and . . . Sinclair Lewis is a perfect example of this pattern. His early writing is going up and up and then, after *Arrowsmith,* total collapse. You find this with Hemingway, too. His early things are miraculous. Then, after *A Farewell to Arms,* what have you got?

You find this with painters, too. I mean, why bother doing another painting that's merely a repetition of what you've done before? The message of a painting is not in the objects in the picture, it's in the exploration of the form. By hanging on to a single form, you become petrified; the life goes out of it.

Let me tell a couple of stories here that follow the pattern of the hero's journey. Think of them as images to meditate on.

The first story I'd like to look at is "The Frog Prince," the very first story in *Grimm's Fairy Tales.* We begin with this little girl—a princess, of course—who has a little golden ball.

Now, gold is the incorruptible metal, and the sphere is the perfect shape. So this is *her*—the ball is the circle of her soul. Now, she likes to go out to the very edge of the forest. This is Germany, where the forest is the abyss, as I've said. She sits there playing, and there's a little pool right near her, a little spring, which is the entrance to the lower world. And there she likes to toss her soul around. She'll just toss the little ball and catch it, toss the ball and catch it, toss the ball and catch it, until, at last, she misses it and it goes down into the pond.

Now, there is the girl's self, her potential, being swallowed by the underworld. When that happens, the power that's down there calls up the little dragon who is the threshold guardian: an ugly little frog. The frog at the bottom of the pool is a kind of fairy-tale dragon.

She has lost the ball and she starts to weep; she's lost her soul. I mean, this is depression, this is loss of energy and joy in life; something essential has slipped out. This sort of loss has a counterpart in the *Iliad,* the theft of Helen of Troy, which sets in motion this whole epic adventure, since the princes and warriors of Greece were obligated to get her back.

Here the little golden ball has dropped and up comes the little frog, the inhabitant of the underworld, who says, "What's the matter, little girl?"

She says, "I lost my golden ball."

Very graciously he says, "I'll get it for you."

"That would be very nice."

Being a reasonable frog, he says, "What will you give me?"

For a boon of the kind she's seeking, you've got to give up something; there's got to be an exchange of some kind. So the little princess says, "I'll give you my gold crown."

He shakes his green head. "I don't want your golden crown."

"I'll give you my pretty silk dress."

"I don't want your pretty silk dress."

"Well," she frets, "what do you want?"

"I want to eat with you at the table and I want to be with you as your playmate and I want to sleep with you in your bed."

Underestimating the frog, she says, "Okay, I'll do that."

The frog dives down and brings up the ball. The fun thing here is that he's the hero, too, on the adventure; he brings up the bauble to give it to her.

She, without so much as a thank-you, takes the ball and goes trotting home.

Well, he comes flopping after, saying, "Wait for me!" Unfortunately, he's very slow, and she gets home well ahead of him, thinking she's left him behind.

Then, that evening at dinner, the little princess and King Daddy and Queen Mommy are having dinner. Now, it seems in that particular palace, the dining table was very close to the front door. They're having a very nice meal, when this wet thing comes flopping up the front steps, and the girl goes a bit pale.

The father says, "What's the matter, dear, what's that?"

She says, "Oh, just a little frog I met."

Being a wise king, he asks, "Did you make any promises?" Now here's the moral principle coming in, the persona complex—you know we've got to correlate all these things.

Of course, the princess is obligated to say that, indeed, she did make a promise.

So the king says, "Open the door and let him in."

So, in hops the frog. The princess is embarrassed and sets up a little place for the frog under the table, but he will have none of this. He says, "No, I want to be on the table; I want to eat out of your golden plate." As you can imagine, that rather spoils dinner for the young lady.

Finally, dinner is finished, and she's going off to bed. Here the frog comes again, flopping up the stairs after her and banging against her door. He says, "I want to come in."

So she opens the door and lets him in.

"I want to sleep in your bed with you."

Freudians love this story.

Well, that's more than she can take. There are several ways of ending this story, the most famous being that she kisses him and he is transformed. But the one I like the best is that she picks him up at this point and throws him against the wall. And the frog cracks open and out steps this beautiful prince with eyelashes like a camel.

What we discover is that he, too, was in trouble. He had been cursed, transformed by a hag into a frog. Now, that's the little boy who hasn't dared to move on into adulthood. She's the little girl who's at the brink of adulthood, and both of them have been refusing it, but each now helps the other out of this neurotic stasis. Of course, they immediately fall in love, swapping anima for animus.

Then, so the story then says, the next morning, after she has introduced him to Daddy and Mommy, after they'd been married, a royal coach comes to the front door. It turns out that he is indeed a prince, and this is his coach, which has come to return him to his kingdom, which had been in desolation from the time of his transformation to a frog. This is the wasteland motif that was a central image in the Grail romances of the Middle Ages. The king is the heart of the land, and while he is incomplete, the land lies devastated.

So the bride and groom get into the coach, and, as they're driving, there's a sound of *bang*. The prince says to the coachman, "What's the matter, Heinrich, what's happened?"

The coachman says, "Well, ever since you've been gone, dear prince, there have been four bands of iron around my heart, and one of them has just now broken."

Then, of course, as they ride along, there are three more bangs, and then the heart of the coachman is beating properly again. Obviously, the coachman himself is symbolic of the land, which requires the prince as its generating and governing power. But the young hero had failed in his duty by refusing the call. He had gone down into the otherworld against his will, but down in the otherworld, he found his little bride. So all is well, if you can pardon the pun.

I like that story particularly because you have both of them in trouble and they're both in the bottom of the well and each rescues the other. And meanwhile, the world up here is waiting for its prince to return.

Another story that follows the pattern in interesting ways comes from the Navaho. It's called "When the Two Came to Their Father," and it was the subject of the very first book I worked on, editing and writing commentary for the anthropologist Maud Oakes.

Now, American Indian stories like this one often feature twin heroes. And one is the active and the other is the contemplative twin—the extrovert and the introvert.

The first young man is named Killer of Enemies. He's the out-turned, aggressive one. The second boy is called Child of the Water. He's the wizard. Their mother, Changing Woman, conceived them both when the sun impregnated her on its way across the sky.

Well, there are monsters round about, and the mother tells them, "Don't go far from the house. You may go eastward, southward, and westward, but don't go north."

Of course, they go north. How are you going to change the situation unless you break the rules? Her proscription is the call to adventure.

They want to go to their father, to get weapons to help their mother and fight all of the monsters. Rainbow Man carries them to the edge of the known world, the threshold. And at each point of the compass, the way is blocked by a threshold guardian: Blue Sands Boy, Red Sands Boy, Black Sands Boy, and White Sands Boy. They flatter and cajole their way past these ogres and tell them they are going to get weapons from their father, the sun; the guardians let them go.

Now they are beyond the realm of the known world. They are in a kind of desert, where there are no features on the landscape at all. They come across a little old lady: her name is Old Age. She says, "What are you doing here, little boys?"

Well, they tell her they are going to their father, the sun. And she says, "That's a long, long way. You'll be old and dead before you get there. Let me give you some advice. Don't walk on my path. Walk off to the right."

Well, they start walking and they forget and they walk on her path. So they find themselves getting tired and old; they have to pick up sticks and then they can't walk at all.

She comes along and she says, "Ah, ah, ah, I told you."

"Well, can't you fix us up?"

So she rubs her hands under her armpits and her loins and rubs the boys' bodies. This gives them life again. Then Old Age says, "Now you go on, and this time stay off my path."

They are wandering along to the side of the road when they see a little smoke coming out of the ground, the fire of Spider Woman. She is another magical helper, an incarnation of the earth mother.

She invites them down into her little hole in the ground and gives them the proper food to give them strength. She tells them what the dangers are on the way; she gives them a magic token, a feather, and sends them on their way.

Then they come to the three trials that block their path: a cactus that pierces; rocks that clash together; and reeds that cut. Well, Spider Woman has given them a feather to hold, and this feather will protect them against all things, so they get safely through.

Finally they come to the ocean that surrounds the world—you see, there are degrees of this unknown world. And now comes the business of crossing the ocean; they do it by flying on their feather. There's a place where ocean and sky come together, and it's blue on blue; and it's right at that point that the sun's house is stationed in the east. Now they come to the place of trials and adventure—these have been just preliminary trials up until now.

Standing by the sun's house is the sun's daughter—the sun is, of course, away on the day's trip. The daughter asks the twins, "Who are you boys?"

They answer, "We are the sons of the sun."

Surprised, she says, "Oh? When my father comes back, he's going to be very angry. I think I had better hide you." So she wraps them in clouds of the four colors and stows them over two different doors.

That evening, the sun arrives and gets off his horse. His shield is the sun disk. Well, he hangs his shield on the wall, and it goes clang clang clang clang clang clang clang clang. Then he turns to his daughter and he says, "Who are those two young men I saw coming in here today?"

She says, "You always told me that you behave yourself when you're going around the world. These two boys say they're your sons."

"Well," he says, "we'll see about that."

So he finds them, takes them down, and then starts an important routine that you find in many, many stories: the father testing the son—or, as in this case, the sons. And he gives them all kinds of brutal treatment. He throws them against great spikes in the four directions. They hold Spider Woman's feather tight. He gives them poison tobacco to smoke. They hold the feather tight. He puts them in a sweathouse to steam them to death, and they hold the feather tight. Finally he says, "You are my sons, so come on into the next room."

There he lays down two buffalo robes, and stands one boy on each. The thunder powers come in, there's a great uproar, and they are given their proper names. He tells them what their names are. They're given their proper height, and he gives them the weapons that they need.

That's the atonement with the father and the achievement of the boon. Now they've got to get home. The sun brings them to the hole in the sky, and when they reach that, he gives them a final exam: what are your names? What's the name of the North Mountain? The East Mountain? The Central Mountain?

They answer all the questions because two little spirits are whispering all the answers in their ears. One is called Black Fly and another is called Little Wind. Now, they tell me that as you're walking along the desert, there's a big fly that comes and sits on your shoulder—perhaps you've seen this. This fly is regarded as the Holy Ghost. This is a visitation of the spirit, so this is what whispers all the answers.

Well, they pass the exam and then go down to the Central Mountain —the *axis mundi*—which to the Navaho is identified with Mount Taylor, in New Mexico. At the base of the mountain is a great lake, and living by the lake is the archetypal monster—you can't kill merely physical monsters until you've killed the archetype. The archetype's name is Big Lonesome Monster. Curiously enough, he, too, is a son of the sun.

The characteristic of monsters is that they mistake shadow for substance. Well, the monster sees the boys reflected in the lake, and he thinks that the reflections in the lake are his enemy. So he decides to drink the lake up and digest them to death. So he drinks the lake up and digests hard, then spits the lake out again. There they are again; they're on the opposite shore, reflected in this thing. The monster does this four times. By that time, even the Big Lonesome Monster is pretty well worn out.

Now, the boys move in then for the kill, and with the sun's help, they destroy Big Lonesome Monster—there you are, Father always loved them best.

Having killed the monster, the boys finally are starting home; they are returning back across the threshold.

Here comes a very, very interesting thing, a little motif that you find in lots of mythologies: the loss of the boon. The twins have to cross the threshold to get back home. They have been in the field of sheer solar power. Now they have to come back to the realm of the female power, where the fierce energy of the sun is tempered to life.

Have you ever wondered why Zeus was always disguising himself when he visited these mortal women? The full blast of a god would kill everything, and then there's no life. You have to have the counterplay of water, you might say, against solar fire.

This is the world in which the heroes will have to function; having accomplished their mythological deed, they now come down to do the actual, practical one. Yet as they cross back over the threshold, they stumble and the weapons that their father gave them shatter—they lose them both.

Then up comes a deity who's called Talking God; he is the masculine ancestor of the female line of the gods, so he represents the two together. His nose is made of a cornstalk; the upper lids of his eyes represent masculine rain, while the lower lids represent female mist. So he's an androgynous figure. He gives them new weapons, new advice. Then they go to work on the monsters that have been rampaging around their home and kill them. And when they have finished that fight with the four great monsters, they are so fatigued that they're about to die.

Then the gods come down and perform a ritual over them that heals them. And what is the ritual? It is the rehearsal of this very story I've just been telling you, the story of their lives. That's what the psychiatrist does when he goes down to find what's wrong with you, why you are out of touch with your unconscious. The gods lead the twins through this little psychodrama and put the hero twins back in touch with the dynamism of the road of their lives.

This ritual was given to Maud Oakes by an old medicine man named Jeff King down in the Navaho country, at the beginning of the Second World War. The United States was inducting Navaho boys into the army because their language was an unbreakable code—the Germans and Japanese didn't have any Navaho speakers. Well, when a boy was drafted, old Jeff King would perform this ritual over him to convert him into a warrior. The rite would last three days and nights, during which time the whole story was reenacted with songs and paintings—there's a whole series of eighteen wonderful sand paintings that show the story. The idea was to turn these sheepherding boys into warriors, because being a soldier requires a different mentality from living in a village.

This is something that we don't do, so you have a lot of crack-ups that are the result of not-very-well-prepared psyches. So here's the function of this myth—it's a warrior myth.

Old Jeff King is buried now in Arlington Cemetery. He was a scout that helped the United States Army when they were fighting the Apaches. He had this old war ceremony that he brought out of the box for the boys that were inducted to war. So he'd give them the use of the ritual in the practical matters of life.

What is the adventure of these Navaho boys? They're moving from a life in a community into action as warriors. They have to undergo a transformation—that's a threshold, and it's one through which they're dragged, you might say, by the draft board.

The Odyssey is just the opposite sort of story. *The Odyssey* is the debriefing of a warrior. He's got to get back home, to leave his warrior ways behind him and return to the female-inflected world of home and bed.

We don't have much in the way of myth today to help us through these transitions. We can turn to the leftover shards of the old myths, or we can try to turn to art.

I saw the *Star Wars* movies recently. George Lucas invited my wife, Jean, and me to his place up in Marin County to see the films because he said they were based on my books, on the idea of the hero journey. Well, I hadn't seen movies for thirty years, so I was just amazed.

This was a surreal experience. In the morning of the first day, we saw *Star Wars.* That afternoon, we saw *The Empire Strikes Back,* and then that evening, we saw *The Return of the Jedi.* And I could see my stuff in there, there's no doubt about that. I ended up a fan, in great admiration of that young man. He has an artist's imagination and a great sense of responsibility to his public that what he is rendering must have value. And with all the galaxies out there to work with, he's got the kind of open field that the early poets used to have. For example, when the Greek Argonauts go up into the Black Sea, where nobody had been, they could meet all kinds of strange monsters and strange people—Amazons and such. It's a blank sheet for the play of the imagination.

As I watched these movies, I realized that he is systematically using the archetypes that he learned about from my books—he says this. For instance, in *The Empire Strikes Back,* Luke Skywalker confronts what he thinks is Darth Vader, the shadow-father figure. He kills the figure and then sees that the face of the machine man is actually his own.

Then, as I've said, at the end of the *Return of the Jedi,* you have the father-atonement motif worked out very explicitly; that's what the whole series is heading for. This series was really a three-act play: the call to adventure; the road of trials; and the final trial, with the reconciliation with the father and the return across the threshold.

It's very gratifying to know that this little book of mine is doing what I wanted it to do, namely to inspire an artist whose work is actually moving in the world. *The Hero with a Thousand Faces* was refused by two publishers; the second one asked me, "Well, who will read it?" Now we know.

Artists are magical helpers. Evoking symbols and motifs that connect us to our deeper selves, they can help us along the heroic journey of our own lives.

It is a popular game among literary critics and graduate students to discuss a particular writer's influences—who they got their ideas and style from. Well, when the operation of creation is in play, an author is surrounded by an ambient of everything he has ever experienced—every childhood accident, every song he's heard, and, too, every book and poem and pamphlet he has read. His creative imagination pulls these things out and puts them into a form.

Now, all these myths that you have heard and that resonate with you, those are the elements from round about that you are building into a form in your life. The thing worth considering is how they relate to each other in your context, not how they relate to something out there—how they were relevant on the North American prairies or in the Asian jungles hundreds of years ago, but how they are relevant *now*—unless by contemplating their former meaning you can begin to amplify your own understanding of the role they play in your life.

In the ascent of the *kuṇḍalinī* serpent up the spine—which is another hero journey, note—the final obstacle to overcome, at the transit from the sixth *cakra* to the seventh, is the barrier between the self and its beloved, the Lord of the Universe—the god that is the world and transcends the world. But what is this line here, below which everything is two, and beyond which there is neither being nor nonbeing? That is our old friend *māyā*.

The word *māyā* comes from the root *mā*, which means "to build or measure forth." *Māyā* has three powers. One power is called the obscuring power; it obscures our understanding of the pure light. The second power is called the projecting power. It converts the pure light into the forms of the phenomenal world as a prism turns white light into colors of the rainbow. These are the powers that turn the transcendent into the temporal, spatial world that we know and all its things.

Now, if you take colors and put them on a disk and spin the colors, they will reveal white again. The colors of this world can be so inflected; they can be arranged in so artful a way that they will let you experience through them the true light. This is called the revealing power of *māyā*—and the function of art is to serve that end. The artist is meant to put the objects of this world together in such a way that through them you will experience that light, that radiance which is the light of our consciousness and which all things both hide and, when properly looked upon, reveal.

The hero journey is one of the universal patterns through which that radiance shows brightly. What I think is that a good life is one hero journey after another. Over and over again, you are called to the realm of adventure, you are called to new horizons. Each time, there is the same problem: do I dare? And then if you do dare, the dangers are there, and the help also, and the fulfillment or the fiasco. There's always the possibility of a fiasco.

But there's also the possibility of bliss.

CHAPTER VII

DIALOGUES[63]

MAN: *You spoke earlier about pyramids and cathedrals. What do you think our contemporary monuments and accomplishments are?*

CAMPBELL: One of the greats was, I think, going to the moon. And, of course, this wasn't done by people asking, "What's the economic value of that?" If you go down that road, economics wins and aspiration loses every time, and all of the fun is gone out of the year—out of mine, at least.

I think the world lives on crazy things. The economics will work themselves out later—you can count on it. There are all sorts of products turning up in our kitchens that are a result of the space program—metals that are easy to cook on and clean, that sort of thing. But it's the scope of the aspiration that really matters.

MAN: *What do you think about the Christ of the Ozarks? (Laughter) They have this huge cross with music playing and floodlights up on the hill there.[64]*

CAMPBELL: Well, someone wants to express his excitement. (Laughter) That's fine. That's what an artist does. And he is attached to an archetypal image. But what does it mean? When Saint Paul says, "I live now; not I, but Christ liveth in me," that's one thing. It's another thing to put the Christ up on a mountain. This is a big problem in life: what do you do with your Christ when he comes along? Do you take that image to yourself and let it become the motivating force for your life, or do you put it up there and make a war cry out of it? This is a very hard problem.

WOMAN: *What do you do, Mr. Campbell? What is your image of God?*

CAMPBELL: It's such fun to answer that question, you know. "Mr. Campbell, what do you do?"

"Oh, I write and read about mythology."

"Oh, isn't that interesting. I've read Bullfinch, and it's so interesting."

"Well," I say, "I'm attracted to mythology a little more deeply than that. Do you believe in God?"

"Well, yes."

"Wonderful. Is it a boy, or is it a girl?"

Alan Watts used to tell the story of the *Apollo* astronaut who came back from space; some smart-aleck reporter asked, since he'd been to heaven, had he seen God? "Yes," answered the astronaut, "and she's black."[65]

So I ask my interlocutor: "How do you feel about that? It's male? Fine. Is he up there, or is he down there? Is there anybody around him? Is he all alone? Is it a rational power? A moral power? Affirmation? Negation? Improvement? Consciousness? Unconsciousness? A personal god? An impersonal power? Do you think of it principally in the feminine or in the masculine form?"

Of course, in the Indian Śakti cult, the goddess is the big thing. In the Jewish male cult, Yahweh is the big thing. You can ask yourself all of those questions. Where does your image of God fit?

For myself, well, Alan Watts once asked me what spiritual practice I followed. I told him, "I underline books."

It's all in how you approach it.

Leo Frobenius describes a wonderful ritual of the Pygmies, a hunting people in the Congo. Frobenius made about twenty expeditions to Africa, and on one of these, his company was joined by three Pygmies, two men and a woman. When they finally ran out of meat, he said to them, "Will you go out and bag a gazelle for us?"

They looked indignantly at him. "Bring a gazelle to you just like that? We have to go through some preparations for this." So he followed them on the preparation. What did they do? They went up a little hill where there was a bald top. They cleared off the scrub, and they drew a picture of a gazelle. And then they had to wait all night, and when the sun rose the next morning, one of these two little men stood with his bow and arrow in the direction that the sun was going to come, and he shot the arrow into the picture of the gazelle so that it hit the gazelle in the neck. And at that same time the woman lifted her arms—you will see just this image on many Neolithic rock drawings, a woman with her arms lifted and the man shooting an arrow. And then they went down and tracked down an actual gazelle. They shot it in the neck.

In other words, it wasn't the man as a personal actor who was doing that but as the agent of the power of life, the power of the sun.

Now, there's the way a rite works—there's something about that business of identifying yourself with something that's happening. There is a story—you may have heard me tell it before—of a samurai. His overlord had been killed, and his vow was, of course, absolute loyalty to this lord. And it was his duty now to kill the killer. Well, after considerable difficulties, he finally backs this fellow in a corner, and he is about to slay him with his *katana,* his sword, which is the symbol of his honor. And the chap in the corner is angry and terrified, and he spits on the samurai, who sheathes his sword and walks away. Now why did he do that? He did that because this action made him angry, and it would have been a personal act to have killed that man in anger, and that would have destroyed the whole event.

It is very much like this hunting act of the Pygmy. This is a mythological attitude. You are acting not in terms of your individual, personal life but with the sense of yourself as the priest, so to say, of a cosmic power which is operating through you, which we all are in circumstances, and the problem is to balance yourself against that and have a personality at the same time.

MAN: *You've talked about transcending dualism, the world of opposites. Is it possible to do that in this life?*

CAMPBELL: There is no experience of life that doesn't have dualism and yet doesn't have the experience of oneness behind the dualism as well. So I would say the primary mythological motif is that of helping you to experience what Jung calls the *coniunctio oppositorum,* the conjoining of opposites. One way or another, they can fuse into each other or they can be held in a beautiful balance to each other—a dance. The pleasure of a couple's dance is that of a pair of opposites in harmonious relationship.

Now, the thing that comes to my mind always when I think of this is a tennis game. You can't have a tennis game without two sides of the net, and if you're going to be affirmative of tennis, you have to be affirmative of the condition of being on only one side of the net at a time. But you have to be firm for that side of the net, or there's no game either. So recognize your own character, your own role of the game, what side of the net you're on, and be *there,* but that doesn't mean that the person on the other side of the net doesn't have the same value as you on this side. This opposition is the game. Do you see what I mean?

Myths may seem to be functioning on quite another level, but let's just take one opposition: Siegfried and Fafner, the dragon that he kills—the typical dragon-killing deed of the hero crossing the threshold. He and the dragon are opposites, but it's only when he has tasted the dragon's blood and integrated the dragon character in himself that he hears the birds sing and knows what their song is saying. You don't get in touch with the nature force that includes both you and the other until you have accepted as part and parcel of yourself the formerly excluded part, that which was seen to be other. It is because of the accidents of your life—your family, your society, the heartache and the thousand natural shocks that human flesh is heir to—that you turned out this way instead of that way. But you have the same potential within you. Jung's psychology makes the very important point that you don't have to *identify* with the other to *assimilate* the other and recognize that what it represents is another aspect of that which you are.

The only mythologies in which you have an absolute duality are those that stem from the Near East after the time of Zoroaster. With Zoroastrianism, you have the idea of a god of light and a god of darkness who are in competition, and their competition has created the world that we have now. And you have to align yourself with the god of light against the god of darkness.

In other traditions, those two powers—light and dark, good and evil—are the right and left arms of one being of beings who transcends the pair of opposites. You can even find hints of this in the Bible, in the books that were composed before the Babylonian exile brought the Jews into contact with Zoroastrian ideas. In Isaiah, the Lord says, "I form the light, and create darkness: I make peace, and create evil: I the Lord do all these things."[66] Now, there's a god who transcends duality. And, my gosh, in his behavior you can see that he does things that, if a human being did them, would be regarded as evil. For example, in the Book of Job, God behaves atrociously—from a human standpoint. At certain points what might be called the *mysterium tremendum et fascinans* comes breaking through, the tremendous aspect of the divine, which is fascinating and at the same time horrific. Normally, Yahweh is the god of a moral order where there is good and there is evil. But look at his justification of his actions to Job, and you realize this is a power beyond morality.

Just remember that before Adam and Eve ate the apple, they knew nothing about good and evil. In fact, knowing the distinction between good and evil is what is called the Fall. So, if you want to get into the condition of Adam and Eve before the Fall, you must go back beyond good and evil again and know that good and evil are the forms through which a transmoral principle operates in the field of time-space, in the tennis game.

Now, if your impulse is to assert your ego and your ego values in such a way that you are destroying other people, for you then to think, I am beyond good and evil and so I can behave this way no matter what happens to other people—you're a dangerous person. You are a sociopath. But if you have already been, as it were, domesticated, civilized, so that not violence and lust but love is your animating principle, then you cannot but realize, as Christ did, that God's rain falls on the just and the unjust, God's light shines on the just and the unjust; if you're going to be as your Father in heaven—wherever that may be—then you must also recognize that what you call just and what you call unjust are not final definitions of those people's values. It doesn't mean that you mustn't fight for your values and be strong for them—I mean, this is the mysticism of warfare: people fight and kill and die for values, but in that fight they realize that the other one is equally justified before the Lord, as it were.

This is in our Western tradition; it's in Christ's own words. But you must realize that all these deep things, all these final things, become translated then into practical, moralizing terms—thou shalts and thou shalt nots—that are good for the society and for the people that are being abducted into society. You're inducted into society first, and then you're abducted into the wisdom of life, which goes a little beyond that, I should say.

In Eden, you couldn't have anything with just Adam there; he was bored, God was bored, the whole thing was bored, until God brought forth what Joyce called the "cutlet-sized consort" from Adam's side. The rib comes out, and the one has become two, and life, time actually, begins with that duad.

This is why I am troubled by some of the things I notice in the young people whom I have been teaching—the idea of the unisex; you know: same hair, same clothes, same activities. You lose tension. I think it is a greater charity to life to maintain the tension than to release it, because vitality comes from tension. The electricity that carries our voices through a telephone wire is both positive and negative; if you didn't have that opposition, there would be no echo.

The important thing, however, is not for the masculine to be the dominant or the feminine to be dominant; what is to be dominant is the *coniunctio oppositorum,* the conjunction of the two.

In a marriage, for example, what is the precious thing? Is it the marriage, or is it Tom, or is it Jane? If Tom thinks it's Tom and Jane thinks it's Jane, you don't have a marriage. But if the two of them, through all their agony of opposition, can maintain the idea that the precious thing is the marriage itself, the precious thing is what lies beyond the pair of opposites, then you've got a good position to start from.

Now, my friend Heinrich Zimmer used to speak of the male-female relationship as a creative opposition, a creative conflict. The balance is in the tension; it's like the tennis game. The tennis game isn't a bad idea. You see, the ball's got to go back and forth, and each player is fighting all the way, so that it's a good game. You know, you let yourself go when you're angry and fighting—my gosh, you wouldn't do very well if you didn't forget that it's a game, that there is another side, and go all the way for your own position. But that doesn't mean that behind all that you don't know the other.

The Zen master Dōgen, the great teacher of a Sōtō sect, said that the duality is recognized, but that does not obstruct the knowledge of the unity. You stress the duality, but duality does not obstruct the realization of the unity. That enriches your humanity.

This is the nature of knightly combat: that two knights ride at each other but each is recognizing the other as a noble knight. The fanatic is a person who has lost that balance and thinks he's right: R-I-G-H-T. And that's a fierce kind of monster to have to face.

WOMAN: *Can the Bible be read in this mythological way? Can the symbols of the Christian and Jewish traditions be read as transcending the field of opposites?*

CAMPBELL: You know, there are these moments in the Bible that you can pull out, and they will help you then to enrich your life. You don't have to throw the Bible away, but you certainly do have to reread it, because the orthodox readings are usually inferior readings—quite literal. That you can have two quite contrary mythologies using the same symbol and thinking of it themselves as being Hebrew or Christian—the orthodox position in both of these traditions is good versus evil, of God and man as separate. But every one of the symbols is susceptible to being read in terms of transcendence of opposites. You've got the Gnostic and kabbalist sects that look at the same symbols with a much more mystical eye. Remember what the Lord says to Isaiah: "I form the light, and create darkness: I make peace, and create evil." Well, that puts the Lord above passive opposites. That's a bigger dimension of God than the one we have in the orthodox traditions.

This is something that comes out in Jesus very strongly, but not in Christianity as it has been practiced. When Jesus says, "Ye have heard that it hath been said, Thou shalt love thy neighbour, and hate thine enemy. But I say unto you, Love your enemies."[67] Love your enemies? Suppose the enemy represents everything that's reprehensible to you. Suppose the enemy is Hitler. Are you capable of that love? If not, are you going to call yourself a Christian?

He must remain your enemy because of your persona system. What you have been taught to regard as good and as evil do not correspond to what he stands for. So you have to stand for what you do stand for. But can you love him? And then the love puts you in the position of seeing both sides of the tennis court, even though you are playing on one side of the net. Do you see what I mean? You're in the position of the umpire now, and yet you've got to play your own side of the net as well. This is a very interesting problem.

Christ says, "Love thine enemies...That ye may be the children of your Father which is in Heaven: for He maketh His sun to rise on the evil and on the good, and sendeth rain on the just and on the unjust."[68] Christ read this as a revelation, a realization of an almost Buddhist sense of oneness with the whole of creation, and with the Creator, whereas in the orthodoxy that revelation is quenched. Jesus says, "I and My Father are one."[69] He was crucified for that by the orthodox community because man and God are not one, but he said they are. Al-Hallaj experienced the same fate nine hundred years later for exactly the same reason.

Then when the church tried to work this thing out, they ended up with the doctrine that Christ is true god and true man. That wasn't what he was saying; he always called himself the son of man. And yet he and the Father are one. It's all there in the book.

WOMAN: *How about the image of Frankenstein? I have a ten-year-old boy, and he is fascinated with Frankenstein.*

CAMPBELL: There are a lot of mythological themes there, and the basic one is the alchemical idea of the homunculus, a creature made by art. Of course, the most noble representation of this is in Goethe's *Faust.* In the first scene of part 2, Faust is at work in his laboratory, bringing forth little Homunculus, the little man made by art in the bottle. Now, what Homunculus symbolizes there is the birth of the new man, the Virgin Birth, and the bottle is the virgin womb. This is man made by art, not by nature, art being a discipline and technique of the spirit rather than of the body.

Now, the alchemists always had the feeling that they were helping nature to bring forth the gold from the gross metal, but what they were really interested in was not so much raw gold as the gold of the spirit. There was no end to this business of the spiritual transportation, where you leave the faults of nature behind. The little hunchback in *Frankenstein* represents the fault of nature, the mistakes and all of that which were thought to have been left behind.

I wonder how many of you have read Samuel Butler's *Erewhon.* This is the story of people who invented a machine, an automaton that will take care of their work for them, just as the gods in the old Semitic tradition created man to tend the garden for them. Now man has created the machines to do the work for him. But just as man in the old stories revolts against the gods, so does the machine revolt against the people of Erewhon; and so does Dr. Frankenstein's creature, who is named, appropriately enough, Adam.

Now, why does this story fascinate us? I think it could fascinate us for a couple of reasons. One reason is that we do have the idea of fashioning a new world: leave the old behind and bring forth a world that does not have all the faults that people over thirty have had. The other thing is that in this world where we accent niceness and goodness and talk about God being love and so forth, we darn well know that there is another side of the equation, and the omitted, the repressed, is always what fascinates us, because our spirits seek to balance.

Jung points out that all you read about in the Gospels is love, love, love. But when you read Paul, all you read about is the terrible thing they are going to do to those sinners. You find this in the Old Testament, too. You read the Psalms, singing the praises of the Lord, and then you turn to Joshua and so on, which are full of delight in the destruction that is going to take place, the jubilation that Nineveh and Jericho and one city after another will be razed to the ground. It is quite something.

MAN: *In Mary Shelley's novel, the monster was not an ugly monster but a beautiful creature. When MGM produced the film, they decided there must be some reason for hating this creature, so he was made ugly. He was a beautiful creature, and it was something within man that caused him to show his other side.*

WOMAN: *But also it's wrong for man to make life....*

CAMPBELL: Only God can make a tree. Of course, as somebody said, "Only God could make a cockroach."

WOMAN: *Can you talk about the woman's hero journey? Is it the same as for a man?*

CAMPBELL: All of the great mythologies and much of the mythic storytelling of the world are from the male point of view. When I was writing *The Hero with a Thousand Faces* and wanted to bring female heroes in, I had to go to the fairy tales. These were told by women to children, you know, and you get a different perspective. It was the men who got involved in spinning most of the great myths. The women were too busy; they had too damn much to do to sit around thinking about stories.

WOMAN: *I don't have any problem identifying with the hero in all aspects. I've been getting in touch with my animus. One of the processes that came up for me was through the Renaissance Fair; I really got interested in knives, and this sense of being the knight and the whole suit of the swords in the tarot and what that power was. So I bought this knife, and for a while I'd just carry it around and, at night, I'd hold it, and I wore it on my skirt and just got in touch with all that masculine energy.*

CAMPBELL: You'd be arrested for that in New York. (Laughter)

WOMAN: *A lot of people didn't understand that, I have to say. (Laughter) I even went into the men's bathroom, to get in touch with that. I went into the stall and closed the door; I could see people's feet under there, but their feet didn't look that much different than the women's feet, except maybe they were a little bit bigger.*

MAN: *Which way were they pointing?*

WOMAN: *What, the knives? (Laughter) I've been playing with the mythological archetypes in my own mind for quite a while, and I am able, I find, to identify just as much with the prince and the king as I am with the princess. In fact, now part of my process is coming back and getting more in touch with the female and the goddess: Isis and Artemis and even the devouring mother, Kālī Ma.*

CAMPBELL: Well, your story is a double one. First you found the male power and that's the knife, but in that you're removed, of course, from the female. And now, you're taking the return journey to integrate this discovery with your female character.

WOMAN: *At first, yes, of course, it felt a little strange and most people didn't understand—I mean, I really got into loving this knife, this holding of this dagger, and then I started meditating on the tarot cards. At first it was the suite of swords and then I got to the knight and then, of course, I could relate real well to the king, but finally coming up with the queen of swords, who is, you know, a wonderful archetype of power, but she is female.[70] At one point, I had a whole collection of different tarot decks. I would take maybe twelve different queens of swords and just look at them and just look at them and hold my damned knife and look at them and hold my knife and look at 'em, hold my knife—to the point where I really internalized that sense of power.*

CAMPBELL: Well, this is a beautiful example of the problem of the relationship of the female to the animus. And as I see the difference, a male going to and finding the place of the knife—that's the instrument of his full power—would not then have the problem of discovering the female in himself. Would *not* have the problem of discovering the female in himself because the feminine factor in the male life and body is slight compared with the feminine factor in your body. Do you see what I mean? It's a greater distance from what the body has given you. And so it's a matter of proportion.

My wife, Jean, has always said that she would have no difficulty, just as you said, in associating with the male hero, because what the male represents is the agent of the feminine power directed toward a certain specific kind of functioning.

However, the male body lacks that recall to nature, to the female nature that there is automatically in the female body. Now, when I was in my twenties I was living with my sister Alice in Woodstock, New York. My sister was a sculptor and her friends were sculptors and so I was living with artists, many of whom were young women. I noticed that one after another, as they approached the age of thirty, the marriage problem came up, even for my sister. This mantra began to take hold of them: got to get married now and have a child and all this kind of thing. And then the divorce followed and it was all just a mess. The art goes to pieces, too, because you can't carry seriously an art career unless you're at it all day long with nothing else. Somehow, this wreckage did not happen with the men. And that's this business —you found the knife, certainly; she found the mallet and chisel. But then the female calls. And when the female calls the male, all he does is go out and get married; that's the female out there, where it naturally is. Do you see what I mean? This is one of the points in the female journey, I would say, that there's a heavier load of given nature to deal with.

I remember reading a Jain text having to do with yoga. Now, Jainist yoga is extreme; the idea is really to cancel nature altogether. They call it kaivalyam—being absolutely isolated from all the calls of the body. This is where vegetarianism is intended to lead, cutting out the killing, the living off of death. No killing, nothing of that kind, except of course yourself; what you're killing is your desire to live. And the goal is to die just at the moment when you are quit of all desire for life, without resentment or anything of the kind. Well, this particular yoga is not recommended for women. There is too much life in their bodies. That just hit me: that much of a summons to life; the whole body tells you, You have disowned me. And the man does not have that problem, at least not to the same extent.

Yes, a woman can follow the hero journey, but there are other calls and there is another relationship asked of you, I would say, to the nature field of which you are the manifestation.

WOMAN: *Another experience that's helped me considerably has been my involvement with shamanism. And in the shaman culture, as you mentioned, there really is no difference between the male and female—they don't see this is a female shaman or male shaman; the shaman is someone with the calling. I have looked at that, and it is very compelling.*

But there was one thing where I do have a little bit of a bone to pick with you, because I do feel that there is a traditional part of you, part of you personally, that does see the female as different from the male, and I'm not sure that I agree.

CAMPBELL: Well, these are two ways of experiencing, I would say, that's all.

I would like for about ten minutes actually to be a female, just to know what the difference is.

Now, it took me a long time to get around to marriage, principally because I knew it would interfere with my reading. (Laughter) That's really true. There was another reason, too: every time I would get really involved with a young woman, I would have the feeling of weight pressing down on me; life was heavy. That heaviness, the feeling that everyone's so goddamned important led me to feel that these little irritations became mountainous problems. I would just get fed up and I'd find myself running out and then, pretty soon, I'd find myself with another young lady, feeling the same weight; whoops, here it is again!

MAN: *Well, attached to women are houses and children and all this other stuff that comes along for the ride. It doesn't have to come with them, but it somehow feels like...*

WOMAN: *But the woman's perspective is exactly the same! (Laughter) I feel exactly that about men! (Laughter) And I'm the one who has to stay in the house! (Laughter) I get out alone and I feel light and free.*

CAMPBELL: My feeling was they always wanted to have fun, and that wasn't my interest at all. (Laughter)

WOMAN: *Well, now, that's true, I'll cop to that.*

WOMAN: *They wanted to have fun and they were heavy.*

CAMPBELL: That's why they needed fun. (Laughter) Well, we do have a consensus here that men and women are different. Or do we?

WOMAN: *I think the women are disagreeing. Well, your conception of how getting married was going to drag you down. My feeling is, God, I have these beautiful, intelligent daughters, and are they going to simply latch onto some man and end up doing the dishes instead of using their potential? Are they going to be washing socks, doing the dishes, dusting the house?*

CAMPBELL: Well, you know, my sister and her friends, they weren't washing the dishes; they were sculpting and so forth. And then their bodies said, "Oh, gee, there's something left out there." If your daughters don't want to wash the dishes, let them stay chiseling something and see how far they can go with it.

WOMAN: *But the body does call. I have a friend that's just a little older than me, very high-powered, very successful, and she said, "The biological clock is running out, should I have a baby? Can I have a baby?"*

CAMPBELL: It's inevitable.

MAN: *It's a question of fulfilling your biologic destiny or your human destiny.*

CAMPBELL: No, that's too big a word. (Laughter)

MAN: *How about a narrower word?*

CAMPBELL: Vocational destiny.

WOMAN: *But is it possible to have both? Is it possible for a woman to be a mother and actualized? And is it possible for a man to be a father and a knight adventurer?*

CAMPBELL: Oh, yes, it is. I'm not saying that this thing has never been resolved, but I'm saying that a typical agony there that makes the actual achievement of the goal different, between a man and a woman, is the strength and weight of the call of the woman's body to have a child, to have whatever else is associated with all this. A man could go on without it.

Of course, the extreme example of men's removal from the life that the woman represents to the world is Mount Athos, the Greek monastery where no woman is allowed. And in the monasteries of the Middle Ages, if a woman came to the door and was brought in, even if she was in great trouble, the doorman was disciplined for letting her come in at all.

The call of the body, this call of nature, is very potent in the woman, in her own life but also as the man experiences her. Now, in *Finnegans Wake,* Joyce takes the Hindu position that woman is the life energy principle. And the man, you might say, just wants to be left alone. And when she goes by, he's activated; she is the activator.

It's interesting: in the north, in the European and Chinese systems, you always hear of yang and yin and that sort of thing. The man is the aggressor and active, and the woman is the receptive and rather passive aspect. Not so in India at all—it's just the opposite. The man psychologically is interested in other things and then this power field goes by and, as Joyce says, "With lipth she lithpeth to him all the time of thuth on thuch and thow on thow." She says, "What a life that was in the last eon. Let's have another eon. . . . Wouldn't it be nice to start the world again?" And the man thinks, "Yes, it would."[71]

So the male gets seduced into the field of action in that way. In India, the female principle is the *śakti,* she's the serpent power that comes up the spine, she's the whole damned flow of energy, in all of its aspects. Now, the great celebration of the goddess in India is the Durgā Pūjā. Durgā is her aspect; she's the eighteen-armed goddess with the swords—when you pick up your knife, you're playing Durgā. *Pūjā* means "ceremony." This festival lasts about three weeks.

The principal image comes from a myth called the *Devī Mahātmya.* In this story, a buffalo-headed yogi, through great concentration, has topped all the gods. None of the gods can overthrow this monster yogi. So they stand in a circle, send their energies back to where they came from, and a great black cloud appears and out of it comes Durgā, the goddess with eighteen arms. In each hand is a symbol of one of the gods. So what the male power represents is merely a specific inflection and definition of the energy that is the female. She's the source of the energy and the male is simply its specification in this, that, or another direction.

So it's much easier, I think, for a woman to identify with the male than it would be for a male who is committed to his lie, to his particular form of abstraction, if you will, to the sphere of action, then to move back to that general thing. It's what the Buddha did, and that was a heroic act of the first order. It's more like a dissolution.

For the woman, it's more a matter of a specification, moving in the other direction. Do you understand what I'm saying? She's bringing herself to a certain point.

MAN: *It seems to me, vis-à-vis the hero journey, that very often a man is going out to find his relationship to life, to life in the larger sense, the apotheosis experience, for instance, the "I am that" experience; in a way it's not so difficult to see a woman on a hero journey, if she doesn't have children. When you said, "What is the female hero journey?" I was thinking of women that I know or women in history, almost as biography, so that you could take certain great women and look at their life as though it were a hero journey and it would probably in terms of—*

WOMAN: *That's not the same thing. That's not the journey.*

MAN: *What?*

WOMAN: *You can have been a very successful woman. It's just a woman working then in this upper, very concrete world; she hasn't taken the journey. Or at least, that's not what we're seeing. The journey is down deep into the psyche, and whether it's a man or a woman, without that journey, you're plainly only living half a life. I mean, that whole mythological dimension hasn't opened. It has nothing to do with what you have achieved in the concrete world.*

MAN: *Well, nothing springs to mind right away, but if you take a woman, for instance, who has both the success in the outer world and has also been going into the mythological world simultaneously, then six of us or ten of us would vote, yeah, that's a hero journey. But I think that the difference is in terms of having children—and I'm never going to have 'em, so I'm just speaking from guesswork here—but there is a way of interpreting childbirth as linking to the eternal life. The female body is hooking into eternal life and somehow withdrawing into that, which is something the male will never experience. And somehow that then changes the journey. Men then have to go out and look for that. They have to go and go through all of those trials and dive into ponds and go through all of this stuff, where the woman just has to be with it. And I think that's part of what changes, that's part of where the female journey differs.*

CAMPBELL: You know, I taught women for thirty-eight years, and it was a very intimate kind of teaching, almost tutorial, so I knew my students very, very well. And then one after another would get married, and they would marry husbands who were interested in and involved in this world, that one, this other one, and those girls would often become advisors to their husbands in their husbands' own field of endeavor without any trouble. In my mind, this is the counterpart of the goddess with the eighteen arms. It's really no problem for a woman, if the situation is one that calls for it, for her to assume the male role. I mean, all she has to take on is a specification of the power that is hers.

But for a man this is a totally different thing; he doesn't have that woman base out of which then to move into another factor. It's a very different psychological problem. Take, for instance, your exercise of identifying with the knife; I would find it very, very difficult to identify with some symbol of a female life that had to do with giving birth to children. I mean, as you say, a man can't give birth. We're not linked to that energy system of life in the same direct way. We're in the field of a specific action function.

So it is in the earliest art, the art of the Cro-Magnon caves and the Venus figurines. The woman is simply a naked form standing there. She's the whole goddamn thing, and the male figures are in specific roles all the time, in specific action functions—hunter, shaman. And it seems to me that image of the great goddess with eighteen arms, she is the story. Each hand has a symbol of one of the gods, but she encompasses them all.

WOMAN: *Joseph, what's striking me now is that the woman's in-built capacity to endure can stick her with the stage of the camel, being loaded.*

CAMPBELL: In *Thus Spake Zarathustra,* Nietzsche gives the three stages of life: the camel gets a load and goes to the desert, becomes a lion, kills the dragon (our old friend, Thou Shalt), and then becomes the self-moving child.[72]

WOMAN: *I wonder if she isn't likely to get stuck at the camel stage because of her ability to endure, where a man, because of his inability to wait and his drive to action, goes to kill a dragon right away, and that's his place of getting stuck. I think these women that stay in the camel state are the ones who, if they don't move on into the lion and beyond, are the ones who get stuck in some of the terrible enantiodromia that you talked about.*

CAMPBELL: After listening to you ladies talking for the past day or two, I had the realization that the characteristic experience of the woman is having to endure something—that this tolerance, this ability to endure, is the prime requirement.

The man has to endure only moments of great pain and struggle and difficulty. This is what you get thrown at in the initiation rites where he's made to endure just out of sight. And I was very much interested. George Catlin, who was among the Mandan Indians in the 1830s, did hundreds of paintings of the Indian people.[73] One series—among the most memorable of the memorable lot—had to do with the initiation of the young men, where they're hung up from the ceiling by spikes through their chests. One of the young men said to him, "Our women suffer, and we must learn to suffer, too." The suffering overtakes women—it is part of the nature of womanhood. Whereas the man has to undertake suffering—it's a big difference.

WOMAN: *And the woman has to get to the point of coming back with that energy, of limiting the suffering, and the man has to learn how to endure longer.*

CAMPBELL: He has got to seek the problem. I've talked about the initiation of boys and girls in these societies. The woman is overtaken by life. When she has her first menstruation, she's a woman.[74] The man never has a comparable experience.

WOMAN: *Except in rites.*

CAMPBELL: That's why the rite has to be so violent. So that he is no longer a little boy. And also he has to be disengaged from his mother. He *has* to be disengaged from his mother.

WOMAN: *But here that never really happens. My brother lived at home until he was twenty-four years old, and he's never really separated from our mother.*

CAMPBELL: Well, I know we have a lot of that. But there are those who do separate. And there are mothers that understand this and assist in the separation. But a clinging mother is a terrible weight on the life of a young man in our culture.

In the primitive and traditional cultures, they are emphatically separated. I was just reading the other day of a Hindu rite in Bengal. Now, this is the extreme condition of the woman-as-camel—she's got to do what her father tells her until she marries, then she's got to do what her husband tells her until he goes off into the forest or dies, and then, if she doesn't throw herself on the funeral pyre, she's got to do what her older son tells her to do. She's never her own boss. And the only strong emotional, valid emotional connection in her life is with her children. So of course there's a ritual to enable the woman to let her son go. This takes place through a series of years. The family chaplain, the guru, comes in and asks the mother for some valuable thing that she must give him. It starts with some of her jewelry, and then certain food she has to give up, and so on. She has to learn to be quit of that which she values. And then comes the time when her little boy is no longer a little boy, he is a man, and by that time, she's learned how to say, The most precious thing in my life can go. That's the initiation rite for the woman, to let go.

But the man has to be systematically withdrawn from the mother's world, put into the men's camp to find his field of action. The girl is overtaken. So the initiation of the girl consists largely of sitting in a little hut at the time of first menstruation realizing, I'm a woman—that's really all it is. The boy has to enact being a man. The girl has to realize that she's a woman. Next thing she knows, in most societies, she's pregnant and now she's a mother.

WOMAN: *And a camel.*

CAMPBELL: Not a camel, necessarily. She's not a camel. That's her field of action—she can go through the whole progression within that field, just as the man does in his field.

WOMAN: *The ideal would be if there could be a transformation where the woman could continue to explore her potential along with motherhood or marriage or whatever she chooses.*

CAMPBELL: But part of the task of having a family is these chores; there isn't a job in the world without chores.

WOMAN: *Well, I agree with that completely.*

CAMPBELL: Dreary, dreary—so what's the problem?

WOMAN: *Yet you've made this point over and over again in your lectures: it's very hard to carry on a creative or a spiritual task when you are constantly distracted.*

CAMPBELL: Well, formerly, having children was the creative job.

WOMAN: *You know, I don't see the hero journey as being involved with whether you do dishes or whether you're present in the boardroom or the battle-field or the library. I think it's a psychological journey, and what you're doing can be creative no matter what it is. If you've resolved the psychological questions inside yourself and integrated that mythical realm, then everything becomes alive. Then there is still a creative aspect in whatever you do. But I don't think it has to do with who does the dishes.*

But I think the journey is psychological, and I think that aspect is pretty similar in the male and female. I know that I identify a lot with the journey that you have written about. But having taken it, it's brought radiance to all my life. If I hadn't taken it, I don't care what I would have become out there; I wouldn't have joy inside. For me, it was finding a ground in the eternal, it was learning to see the world becoming metaphor, it was seeing things differently.

CAMPBELL: When I was teaching these young women, I wasn't thinking of turning them into philologists, you know, or historians. And so, what was I giving them this stuff for? There are lots of ways of using the material. My thought was this: the majority are going to get married, are going to have children, are going to give themselves to these daily chores, which were comparable to my daily chores teaching them, which was no fun either, after the first excitement. (Laughter) But my thought was, they will have a family, and there will come a time when they're in their fifties and their family will begin to go off, like that poor Bengali lady's, and there they will be.

So my intention was to give them this spiritual method for how to read the world in terms of the second half of life journey, and that was it. And that was a long time ago. I know these women now, twenty years, thirty years, forty years later, and unanimously, I hear, this worked. This is something that is now feeding this aspect of each woman's life.

Now you have this problem, too: your job has taken a hell of a lot out of you. Washing dishes can be pretty exhausting. And here you are at an age when you think that life should have more in it. That's the problem—you're thinking about it, do you see?

Now, the other thing is, anyone who gets married is going to have this problem. Because a household weighs on you whether you're male or female. If you're going to enjoy, as I have enjoyed, this eagle flight of the spirit without responsibility, then you should have known that a long time ago and not gotten married. In the woman's case, when she knows it a long time ago and she doesn't get married, thirty comes, and more often than not she wants to get married after all.

WOMAN: *Even if you're not married, there's still dishes to wash.*

CAMPBELL: You bet your life. All life has drudgery to it.

WOMAN: *I mean, some people call it shit work, but I like to think of it more as a Zen thing. I mean, there are certain things that have to be done. There are vegetables that have to be washed so you can eat.*

CAMPBELL: Yes. In Zen, however, even while you're washing the dishes, that's a meditation, that's an act of life. It's not a chore, and it's not what you've just been calling it.

Sometimes the drudgery itself can become part of the hero deed. The point is not to get stuck in the drudgery but to use it to free you.

Now, the adventure is always reckless. There's always a factor of recklessness in it. And that goes even for the simple things I do in rewriting a book. There is a very interesting letter from the German poet Schiller to a young writer who was suffering from what's called writer's block.[75] That's the refusal of the call for the writer. Schiller said, "The problem with you is, you bring the critical factor in before the lyric factor has had a chance to express itself." In literature, we spend our youth studying Shakespeare and Milton, picking over their genius and even criticizing them in some cases. Then we start to write our own pitiful little poem, and we think, Oh, my God, out!

When I'm writing, I think of the whole academic world; I know what they think, and they don't think what I think. I just have to say, Let the guillotine come down; you've got me, kid, but you're gonna get this message. I always feel as though I were going through a Simpeglades that's just about to close, but I get through before I let that thought come to me. And it's a very strange feeling of holding—actually, intellectually, holding—that door open to get this thought out. Now that's, *that's* the way to do it. Don't think about the negative side. There are going to be negatives and they are going to come down and that's like washing dishes, you know? You've got to hold the door open to do anything that hasn't been done before. You have to do your thing, you have to hold all the criticism in abeyance. I'm sure that that's an experience that everyone has in life. In writing, you have it all the time in a minor way, getting that sentence out.

WOMAN: *Because everything else is direction from without.*

CAMPBELL: Everything else. This is killing the dragon. Sometimes the dragon comes carrying a red pencil, and sometimes he comes clattering in with loads of dirty dishes in your place. (Laughter)

I want to hold that—it's a beautiful image. The dragon with a whole dishwashing machine on his body.

WOMAN: *In a way, then, you're saying that the hero may not answer the call because he feels he has a duty to his home. And the female is just the same thing, only her duty might be doing the dishes and the man's duty might be taking care of, I don't know, bringing home the bacon, whatever you want to call it.*

CAMPBELL: At the moment of his achieving *nirvāṇa*, the Buddha was faced with three temptations. The Lord of Lust, Kāma, paraded three beautiful girls before him; their names were Desire, Fulfillment, and Regrets. Well, the Buddha no longer identified himself with his ego. He was identified with the Universal Self, the consciousness, which is in them too. So he wasn't moved; I mean he was in that still point. Then Kāma turns himself into the Lord Fear, Māra, and he throws at the Buddha all the weaponry of a terrific army. The Buddha is no person anymore, and so he's not afraid. He has identified with everything that happens, so insignificant little phenomena like swords and spears can't affect him. And then comes the third temptation. That's the one you just spoke of—dharma, or duty. "Young man seated under this tree, you are a prince! Why are you not governing your people? Why are you not on the throne where you belong?" Well, the Buddha was not going to be moved by that, either. Reaching down with his finger, he touches the earth. He calls the earth, nature itself, to witness that he's in the right place, he's in the central part of the world. And he has performed his duties.

WOMAN: *Right, you have to have washed the dishes or made the money.*

CAMPBELL: Yes, he has performed those tasks, and now he's free. Remember me talking about the *kuṇḍalinī?* The *cakras* of the pelvis are those of clinging to life, of begetting, and of winning—they're *cakras* one, two, and three. And these are what we share with animals. And then the heart *cakra* is the awakening, the opening of the spiritual dimension; everything below is metaphoric of the mystery. And once you have got that point, then these powers becomes spiritualized. The very doing of the things that are of the first three *cakras* becomes the realization of the top three, *cakras* five, six, and seven.

When you know, from the heart in the middle, this is when you bring that factor of love in. As long as the dishes aren't it, you're just trapped in the chore. When you love the dishes and you think about what they mean in your life, when they're your family's food, sustenance, and all, then it's all transformed into metaphor and you're free. And the whole idea of the Bodhisattva is, there is no difference in visual action, in what is seen in action between bondage and release. Two people performing the same act: one is bound, the other's free. Of course, the extreme example is chores that are put on you when you're in prison. But there are histories of saints that have found the transcendent even there.

But the simple tasks of our life, when you're doing them because they're a function or factor in the life that you love and have chosen and have given yourself, then they don't weigh you down.

WOMAN: *I feel like Psyche here, sitting here sorting out between peas and beans, looking to sift out of what has been said, and what the implications for a heroine's journey might be.*

CAMPBELL: Yes.

WOMAN: *And one thing that has occurred to me is that, it is different from the hero's journey, that perhaps its element is time, where the hero's is space. It is this matter of endurance, staying there and sitting it out. Working it through, not sitting it out. Working on it, working on it. Going deeper and deeper, getting clearer and clearer. Whereas for the man, the field of action moves out into what you called the Forest Adventurous. The hero is usually a young man in the hero's journey thing. It isn't usually the middle-aged man, is it?*

CAMPBELL: Yes, it's usually a young man.

WOMAN: *Yes, right.*

CAMPBELL: In *The Odyssey,* you'll see three journeys. One is that of Telemachus, the son, going in quest of his father. The second is that of the father, Odysseus, becoming reconciled and related to the female principle in the sense of male-female relationship, rather than the male mastery of the female that was at the center of *The Iliad.* And the third is of Penelope herself, whose journey is exactly what you're describing: endurance. Out in Nantucket, you see all those cottages with the widow's walk up on the roof: when my husband comes back from the sea. Two journeys through space and one through time.

WOMAN: *Was your point, which maybe was an interesting one, that the hero's journey is usually a young man, where a heroine's journey is maybe a more mature place, where she's passed the dishwashing and the baby making?*

WOMAN: *What about women who don't have babies?*

CAMPBELL: Well, my wife is one. She's a dancer and a choreographer. And Jean worked with Martha Graham, who is nothing but a dancer. Now she's ninety years old but still going, still an artist. The calamity to Martha came when her art was no longer possible, because her body was her instrument. When she couldn't do it, that was a terrific psychological crisis. Jean had the idea of dance as *part* of her life, so that now, when dancing herself is impossible because her body can't do it, she's able to handle this. And always it was her life, not her art, that was the number one thing.

WOMAN: *So she has had her own hero's journey?*

CAMPBELL: She's had an elegant career.

WOMAN: *How does she relate that? Does she think of her career as a hero's journey? Or a heroine's journey, for that matter?*

CAMPBELL: Let's say the mythology's helped a bit. And she had a husband who was willing to help her see it happen.

NOTES

EDITOR'S FOREWORD

1   See p. 112.

INTRODUCTION

2   The majority of the introduction is from a section of a lecture that Campbell gave during 1981 (L965 in the Joseph Campbell Foundation archives). The discussion of the concept of "following your bliss" was drawn from a question-and-answer session from a lecture on April 23, 1983, entitled "The Experience of Mystery" (L830).

3   Karlfried Graf Dürckheim (1896–1988) was a German aristocrat who served as a diplomat in Japan. His exposure to Zen Buddhism and Taoism in East Asia opened up new avenues of thinking for him. When he returned to Europe, he followed an intellectual path that paralleled Joseph Campbell's own in many ways, exploring comparative myth and its corollaries in spiritual practice and Jungian depth psychology. With Maria Hippius, who eventually became his wife, he founded a center for spiritual psychology.

Carl Gustav Jung (1875–1961) was one of the great innovators in twentieth-century psychology. For more on his biography and work, see the chapters "Myth and the Self" and "Personal Myth."

Erich Neumann (1905–1960) was a student of Jung's and a psychologist. Both men explored the connections between mythology and psychology.

4   For further discussion of Joyce's theories regarding proper and improper art, see Joseph Campbell, *The Inner Reaches of Outer Space: Metaphor as Myth and as Religion* (Novato, Calif.: New World Library, 2002), pp. 90–91ff.

5   Lao-tzu, *Tao-te Ching,* trans. Gai-Fu Fung and Jane English (New York: Vintage Books, 1997), p. 1.

6   Waldemar Bogoras, "The Chuckche, Material Culture," *Memoirs of the American Museum of Natural History,* vol. 11, part 1 (New York: G.E. Stechert and Co., n.d.).

7   Gareth Hill et al., *The Shaman from Elko: Festshrift for Joseph L. Henderson, M.D.* (San Francisco: The Jung Society of San Francisco, 1978).

8   Alberto M. de Agostini, *I miei viaggi nella Terra del Fuoco* (Turin: Cartografia Flli. de Agostini, 1923).

9   For more on Campbell's trip to India and East Asia, see Joseph Campbell, *Baksheesh & Brahman: Asian Journals—India,* Robin and Stephen Larsen and Antony Van Couvering, eds. (Novato, Calif.: New World Library, 2002), and *Sake & Satori: Asian Journals—Japan,* David Kudler, ed (Novato, Calif.: New World Library, 2002).

10 James Joyce, *Finnegans Wake* (New York: Penguin Books, 1982), p. 230.

11 Epistle of Paul to the Galatians, 2:20.

12 This concept is a tenet of the nondualistic Advaita Vedanta sect founded by Śankara, circa 800 A.D.

13 The friend was John Moffitt, Jr., whom Campbell met at the Ramakrishna-Vivekananda Center in New York. They each assisted Swami Nikhilananda in translating works for the mission: Campbell edited Nikhilananda's translation of the Upaniṣads, while Moffitt helped translate *The Gospel of Sri Ramakrishna* and Śankara's *Self-Knowledge.* Moffitt is one of very few Westerners to take the vows of a Ramakrishna sunnyasin, which he did in 1959 under the name Swami Atmaghananda.

Moffitt wrote a book detailing his experiences as a holy man in two traditions: *Journey to Gorakhpur: An Encounter with Christ beyond Christianity* (New York: Holt, Rinehart and Winston, 1972).

For more on Swami Nikhilananda and the Vedanta Society, see Joseph Campbell, *Baksheesh & Brahman: Asian Journals—India,* passim.

CHAPTER I

14 This chapter is drawn largely from a lecture delivered May 9, 1968, at Amherst College, entitled "The Necessity of Myth" (L196), a recording of which is available as the fourth part of *The Joseph Campbell Audio Collection,* vol. IV: *Man and Myth.* Part of this section is drawn from a lecture delivered April 17, 1969, at the University of Vermont, entitled "The Necessity of Myth" (L250).

15 Arthur Schopenhauer, "On the Sufferings of the World," *Studies in Pessimism: A Series of Essays,* trans. T. Bailey Saunders, M.A. (London: Swan, Sonnenschein & Co., 1892). Found at http://etext.library.adelaide.au/s/schopenhauer/arthur/pessimism/chapter1.html.

16 Sir Baldwin Spencer, *Native Tribes of Central Australia* (New York: Dover Publications, 1968).

CHAPTER II

17 This chapter is based primarily on a lecture entitled "Man and Myth" that Campbell delivered on October 16, 1972, at the Canadian university Loyola of Montréal (L435). An audio-recording has been released as part of *The Joseph Campbell Audio Collection,* vol. IV: *Man and Myth.* A monograph, also entitled *Man and Myth,* which was based both on this lecture and on a seminar entitled "Imagination and Relation to Theological Enquiry" (L436), was released by the Department of Theological Studies of Loyola of Montréal (Montreal: Editions Desclée & Cie/Les Editions Bellarmin, 1973).

18 The first part of this chapter is drawn from L250. See note 14.

19 Angelus Silesius, *The Angelic Verses: From the Book of Angelus Silesius,* Frederick Franck, ed. (Boston: Beacon Point Press, 2000).

20 Steven Fanning, *Mystics of the Christian Tradition* (New York: Routledge, 2001), p. 103.

21 The exploration of this idea serves as a central theme in both Joseph Campbell, *Thou Art That: Transforming Religious Metaphor,* Eugene Kennedy, ed. (Novato, Calif.: New World Library, 2001), and Campbell, *The Inner Reaches of Outer Space: Metaphor as Myth and as Religion.*

22 This statement—which Campbell would have admitted was controversial—is indicative of a question that would occupy much of his later scholarship. There are, to this day, arguments among social scientists about whether civilizations developed globally through diffusion (as Campbell here posits), convergences, or parallelism. See Campbell, *The Historical Atlas of World Mythology,* vol. 2, part 1 (New York: Alfred van der Marck Editions, 1988), pp. 20ff, and Campbell, "Mythogenesis," *The Flight of the Wild Gander* (Novato, Calif.: New World Library, 2002), passim.

23 The Book of Leviticus, 17:6.

24 Genesis 1:26.

25 Minnehaha was actually a character from Dakota Sioux myth rather than the Blackfoot legend. Her story was made famous by Longfellow's poem "The Song of Hiawatha," which Campbell and most Americans of his generation would have known well. He is therefore using her name jokingly here, which is clear from his tone in the lecture.

26 Leo Frobenius, *Paideuma* (Frankfurt am Main: Frankfurter societät-druckerei, 1928).

27 For more discussion of these themes, see Campbell, *Thou Art That,* pp. 15, 66, 111–112.

28 The Book of Joshua, 1:5.

29 Genesis 3:19.

30 Thomas Aquinas, *Summa contra gentiles,* book 1, chapter 3.

31 Chāndogya Upaniṣad, chapter 12.

32 The exploration of this idea is the central thesis of Joseph Campbell, *Myths of Light: Eastern Metaphors of the Eternal,* David Kudler, ed. (Novato, Calif.: New World Library, 2003).

CHAPTER III

33   The following chapters are based primarily on a lecture entitled "Overview of Western Psychology: Freud and Jung" that Campbell delivered in 1962 at the Foreign Service Institure (L47); on two lectures entitled "Living Your Personal Myth," one of which Campbell delivered on November 17, 1972, at the Analytical Psychiatrists' Club of New York (L441) and the other of which he delivered on May 3, 1973, at the University of Arkansas, Fayetteville (L483); and on a week-long symposium, also entitled "Living Your Personal Myth," that Campbell led at the Esalen Institute in Big Sur, California, from March 16 through March 20, 1973 (L468–L472).

CHAPTER IV

34   This chapter and that following are based on L441, L468–L472, and L483. See note 33.

35   Campbell is commenting on perceived, acculturated differences between the genders. For a deeper exploration of his thoughts on the differences between the genders, see pp. 145–159.

36   The Gospel According to Matthew, 7:1.

37   This is an epigram by an Oxford student and latter-day satirist, Tom Brown, c. 1680. Reputed to have been written as part of a punishment meted out by the dean of Brown's college, Dr. John Fell, it was a translation of an epigram by the Roman poet Martial: *Non amo te, Sabidi, nec possum dicere quare; / Hoc tantum posso dicere, non amo te.* This only goes to show that shadow projection has been with us for quite some time.

38   First Letters of St. Paul to the Corinthians, 13:7.

39   Thomas Mann, *Tonio Kröger,* David Luke, trans. (New York: Bantam Modern Classics, 1990).

40   Thomas Mann, "Little Herr Friedmann," *Death in Venice and Other Tales,* Joachim Neugroschel, trans. (London: Penguin, 1998).

CHAPTER V

41   C. G. Jung, *The Portable Jung,* ed. Joseph Campbell (New York: Viking, 1971), p. xxi.

42   *The Portable Jung,* pp. xxi–xxii.

43   *The Inner Reaches of Outer Space: Myth as Metaphor and as Religion.*

44   The Gospel According to Matthew, 10:39.

45   "En un cuaderno de *La Critica* cita Croce la definitión gue un italiano da del *latoso:* es—dice—el que nos quita la soledad y no nos da la compañía." José Ortega y Gasset, *Obras completas* (Madrid: Talleres Gráficos, 1957), p. 378.

46   For further discussion of *kundalinī* yoga and the sacred syllable *aum,* see Joseph Campbell, *Myths of Light: Eastern Metaphors of the Eternal,* pp. 27–38; *The Inner Reaches of Outer Space,* pp. 36–37, 71–72; and *The Mythic Image* (Princeton, N.J.: Princeton University Press, 1981), pp. 331–87.

47   Henry Adams, *Mont-Saint-Michel and Chartres* (New York: Penguin, 1986).

48   For a deeper discussion of this concept, see Joseph Campbell, *Mythic Worlds, Modern Words: Joseph Campbell on the Art of James Joyce*, Edmund L. Epstein, PhD, ed. (Novato, Calif.: New World Library, 2004), pp. 19–25.

49   This is Campbell's liberal translation of a passage from Dante Alighieri, *Vita nuova*, chapter 2. The full Italian passage reads as follows:

> *In quello punto dico veracemente che lo spirito de la vita, lo quale dimora ne la secretissima camera de lo cuore, cominciò a tremare sì fortemente, che apparia ne li menimi polsi orribilmente; e tremando disse queste parole: "Ecce deus fortior me, qui veniens dominabitur michi." In quello punto lo spirito animale, lo quale dimora ne l'alta camera ne la quale tutti li spiriti sensitivi portano le loro percezioni, si cominciò a maravigliare molto, e parlando spezialmente a li spiriti del viso, sì disse queste parole: "Apparuit iam beatitudo vestra." In quello punto lo spirito naturale, lo quale dimora in quella parte ove si ministra lo nutrimento nostro, cominciò a piangere, e piangendo disse queste parole: "Heu miser, quia frequenter impeditus ero deinceps!"*

50   *Bhairavānanda* is an epithet for Śiva. It is also a title for initiates in certain Tantric sects.

51   Immanuel Kant, *Prolegomena zu einer jeden künftigen Metaphysik, die als Wissenschaft wird auftreten können*, par. 36–38.

CHAPTER VI

52   The following chapter is based primarily on a two-day section of a longer symposium, entitled "Explorations," that Campbell led at the Esalen Institute in Big Sur, California, from November 16 through March 20, 1983 (L1183–L1185).

53   The opening paragraphs of this chapter were drawn from L472. See note 34.

54   Arthur Schopenhauer, "Über die anscheinende Absichtlichkeit im Schicksale des Einzelnen" (Leipzig: Ed. Frauenstaedt, 1851). Campbell read this essay in the original: the title he gives is his own translation from the German. The English translation of the essay appears in E. F. J. Payne, ed., *Six Long Philosophical Essays*, vol. 1, *Parerga and Paralipomena* (Oxford: Clarendon Press, 2000) pp. 199ff.

55   Joseph Campbell, *Myths to Live By* (New York: Penguin, 1983).

56   Joseph Campbell, *The Hero with a Thousand Faces* (Princeton, N.J.: Princeton University, 2004, centennial ed.).

57   Joseph Campbell, *The Historical Atlas of World Mythology*, vol. 1, *The Way of the Animal Powers* (New York: Alfred van der Marck Editions, 1983).

58   T. S. Eliot, "The Hollow Men," *The Waste Land and Other Poems* (New York: Signet, 1998).

59   This meeting is chronicled in Campbell's journal of his trip to India, *Baksheesh & Brahman: Asian Journals—India*, pp. 277–78.

60   Most notably, Jung's last completed work was an exploration of the symbolism of the *hieros gamos* in myth and alchemy: *Mysterium Coniunctionis*, 2d ed., vol. 14, *The Collected Works of C. G. Jung* (Princeton, N.J.: Princeton University Press, 1977).

61   Joseph Campbell and Henry Morton Robinson, *A Skeleton Key to Finnegans Wake* (San Francisco: Harcourt Brace Jovanovich, 1988).
62   To read this article and its follow-up, "Skin of Whose Teeth? Part II," as well as Campbell's thoughts on the novels of James Joyce, see Campbell, *Mythic Worlds, Modern Words.*

PART IV

63   The questions and answers in this chapter are drawn from the lectures from which the bulk of this volume was drawn.

CHAPTER VII

64   The Christ of the Ozarks is a large statue of Christ with outstretched arms that stands on Magnetic Mountain near Eureka Springs, Arkansas. Sixty-seven feet tall and weighing almost a million pounds, the statue was built at the behest of Gerald L. K. Smith, a fundamentalist preacher who was described as "the most prominent anti-Semite in America" from the 1940s until his death in 1977. Smith is buried at the base of the statue. See Michael Barkhun, *Religions and the Racist Right: The Origins of the Christian Identity Movement,* rev. ed. (Chapel Hill, N.C.: University of North Carolina Press, 1966).
65   Alan Watts, "Images of God," *The Tao of Philosophy,* audio ed. (San Anselmo, Calif.: Electronic University Publishing, 1995).
66   The Book of Isaiah, 45:7.
67   The Gospel According to Matthew, 5:43–44.
68   The Gospel According to Matthew, 5:44–45.
69   The Gospel According to John, 10:30.
70   For an in-depth exploration of the archetypal symbolism of the tarot deck, see Joseph Campbell, *The Hero's Journey: Joseph Campbell on His Life and Work* (Novato, Calif.: New World Library, 2003), pp. 179–83. Also see Richard Roberts, *Tarot Revelations* (Fairfax, Calif.: Vernal Equinox Press, 1987), a Jungian exploration of the Waite-Rider deck with a foreword by Joseph Campbell.
71   This is Anna Livia Plurabelle and Henry Chimpden Earwicker from James Joyce, *Finnegans Wake,* p. 23.
72   Friedrich Nietzsche, *Thus Spoke Zarathustra: A Book for All and None,* Walter Kaufmann, trans. (New York: Modern Library, 1995), pp. 25–28.
73   George Catlin (1796–1872) was a painter who lived with, studied, and painted the native people of the Upper Missouri during the 1830s.
74   See Joseph Campbell, *The Masks of God,* vol. 1: *Primitive Mythology* (New York: Penguin USA, 1991), p. 372.
75   Friedrich Schiller (1759–1805) was a leading German poet, critic, and playwright. He is best known as the author of the dramas *Don Carlos* and *Maria Stuart* and "The Ode to Joy," which Ludwig von Beethoven famously set to music in his *Ninth Symphony.*

A JOSEPH CAMPBELL BIBLIOGRAPHY

Following are the major books authored and edited by Joseph Campbell. Each entry gives bibliographic data concerning the first edition. For information concerning all other editions, please refer to the mediagraphy on the Joseph Campbell Foundation Web site (www.jcf.org).

AUTHOR

Where the Two Came to Their Father: A Navaho War Ceremonial Given by Jeff King. Bollingen Series 1. With Maud Oakes and Jeff King. Richmond, Va.: Old Dominion Foundation, 1943.

A Skeleton Key to Finnegans Wake. With Henry Morton Robinson. New York: Harcourt, Brace & Co., 1944.

The Hero with a Thousand Faces. Bollingen Series XVII. New York: Pantheon Books, 1949.

The Masks of God, 4 vols. New York: Viking Press, 1959–1968. Vol. 1, *Primitive Mythology,* 1959. Vol. 2, *Oriental Mythology,* 1962. Vol. 3, *Occidental Mythology,* 1964. Vol. 4, *Creative Mythology,* 1968.

The Flight of the Wild Gander: Explorations in the Mythological Dimension. New York: Viking Press, 1969.*

---

* Published by New World Library as part of *The Collected Works of Joseph Campbell.*

Myths to Live By. New York: Viking Press, 1972.

The Mythic Image. Bollingen Series C. Princeton, N.J.: Princeton University Press, 1974.

The Inner Reaches of Outer Space: Metaphor as Myth and as Religion. New York: Alfred van der Marck Editions, 1986.*

The Historical Atlas of World Mythology:
   Vol. 1, *The Way of the Animal Powers.* New York: Alfred van der Marck Editions, 1983. Reprint in 2 pts. Part 1, *Mythologies of the Primitive Hunters and Gatherers.* New York: Alfred van der Marck Editions, 1988. Part 2, *Mythologies of the Great Hunt.* New York: Alfred van der Marck Editions, 1988.
   Vol. 2, *The Way of the Seeded Earth,* 3 pts. Part 1, *The Sacrifice.* New York: Alfred van der Marck Editions, 1988. Part 2, *Mythologies of the Primitive Planters: The Northern Americas.* New York: Harper & Row Perennial Library, 1989. Part 3, *Mythologies of the Primitive Planters: The Middle and Southern Americas.* New York: Harper & Row Perennial Library, 1989.

The Power of Myth with Bill Moyers. With Bill Moyers. Ed. Betty Sue Flowers. New York: Doubleday, 1988.

Transformations of Myth through Time. New York: Harper & Row, 1990.

The Hero's Journey: Joseph Campbell on His Life and Work. Ed. Phil Cousineau. New York: Harper & Row, 1990.*

Reflections on the Art of Living: A Joseph Campbell Companion. Ed. Diane K. Osbon. New York: HarperCollins, 1991.

Mythic Worlds, Modern Words: On the Art of James Joyce. Ed. Edmund L. Epstein. New York: HarperCollins, 1993.*

Baksheesh & Brahman: Asian Journals—India. Eds. Robin and Stephen Larsen and Antony Van Couvering. New York: HarperCollins, 1995.*

The Mythic Dimension: Selected Essays 1959–1987. Ed. Antony Van Couvering. New York: HarperCollins, 1997.

Thou Art That: Transforming Religious Metaphor. Ed. Eugene Kennedy. Novato, Calif.: New World Library, 2001.*

Sake & Satori: Asian Journals—Japan. Ed. David Kudler. Novato, Calif.: New World Library, 2002.*

Myths of Light: Eastern Metaphors of the Eternal. Ed. David Kudler. Novato, Calif.: New World Library, 2003.*

Editor

Books Edited and Completed from the Posthuma of Heinrich Zimmer:

Myths and Symbols in Indian Art and Civilization. Bollingen Series VI. New York: Pantheon, 1946.

The King and the Corpse. Bollingen Series XI. New York: Pantheon, 1948.

Philosophies of India. Bollingen Series XXVI. New York: Pantheon, 1951.

The Art of Indian Asia. Bollingen Series XXXIX, 2 vols. New York: Pantheon, 1955.

The Portable Arabian Nights. New York: Viking Press, 1951.

Papers from the Eranos Yearbooks. Bollingen Series XXX, 6 vols. Edited with R. F. C. Hull and Olga Froebe-Kapteyn, translated by Ralph Manheim. Princeton, N.J.: Princeton University Press, 1954–1969.

Myth, Dreams and Religion: Eleven Visions of Connection. New York: E. P. Dutton, 1970.

The Portable Jung. By C. G. Jung. Translated by R. F. C. Hull. New York: Viking Press, 1971.

My Life and Lives. By Rato Khyongla Nawang Losang. New York: E. P. Dutton, 1977.

INDEX

A

abortion, 10
Abraham (biblical figure), 82
the absolute, 56
Actaeon, 117
active door, 115
Adam (biblical figure), 38, 72, 141, 142
Adams, Henry, 92
Adler, Alfred, 63–64
adolescence, 61
Adonis, 34
Advaita Vedana sect, 162n.12
adventure, call to, 113–14
    See also hero journey/adventure
Aeschylus: *Agamemnon*, 39
aesthetic arrest, 99
Agamemnon (Aeschylus), 39
Age of Reason, 20

ahiṁsā (nonviolence), 5
Ahura Mazda, 6
alchemists, 144
allegory, xvii
ambivalence, 49
American Indian culture, obliteration of, 99–100
ānandamaya-kośa (sheath of bliss), xxi, xxii
Angelus Silesius, 23
Angra Mainyu, 6
anima/animus (female/male ideal in the masculine/feminine unconscious), 75–80, 82, 116–17, 145–47
animals, spiritual development of, 90–91
annamaya-kośa (food sheath), xx, xxii
Apache Indians, xviii

171

caste system, 9, 56–58
categories of thought, 39–40
Catholic Church, xxv, 8
Catlin, George, 153, 166n.73
Celtic gods, 20
Chāndogya Upaniṣad, 40
Chartres Cathedral, 92
China, 36, 39
Chinese medicine, xvii
Christ
    blasphemy of, 41
    the Cross as threshold for re-
        uniting with God, 116, 118
    death of, and our eternal life, 34
    humanity/divinity of, 41–42
    images of, 137–38
    as Incarnation of God, 92
    vs. Jesus, 23
    on loving your enemies,
        143–44
    on sacrificing oneself to one's
        myth, 89
Christianity
    creator vs. creature in, 40
    vs. European individualism,
        20, 24
    goddesses absent in, 38–39
    historicity of symbols of,
        42, 88
    Virgin Birth, 88, 93–94, 117
    See also Bible; Christ
Chukchi people (Siberia), xviii–xix
civilizations, global development
    of, 163n.22
communication, 91
comparisons, period of, 19
compassion, 76–78, 80

compulsiveness, 64
conjoining of opposites, 139–40
conscience, 49
consciousness
    of Buddha, xxii, 157
    and life, 3–4, 103
    as pointing toward transcen-
        dence, xxiii, 162n.12
contraception, 8–9
Copernican cosmology, 7–8
cosmic cycle, 39
cosmological function of mythol-
    ogy, 7–8, 25, 55
cosmos and ego, 96
counterculture, 121
Cousins, Norman, 122, 123
Cross of the Ozarks (Magnetic
    Mountain, Ark.), 137–38,
    166n.64
Crucifixion, 34, 118
cycle of life, 80–81, 107–8, 152

D

Dante Alighieri, 107–8
    The Divine Comedy, 8–9, 103
    Vita nuova, 98–99
de Agostini, Alberto, xix
death
    crossing threshold to, 115–16
    and ego, 96
    hunting people's view of, 27
    life from, 28–32, 34
    religious view of, 17
decrepitude, 108
deities. *See* gods
dependency, psychological, 11–12,
    51–52

ABOUT THE AUTHOR

Around one hundred years ago, on 26 March 1904, Joseph John Campbell was born in White Plains, New York. Joe, as he came to be known, was the first child of a middle-class Roman Catholic couple, Charles and Josephine Campbell.

Joe's earliest years were largely unremarkable; but then, when he was seven years old, his father took him and his younger brother, Charlie, to see Buffalo Bill's Wild West Show. The evening was a high point in Joe's life; for, although the cowboys were clearly the show's stars, as Joe would later write, he "became fascinated, seized, obsessed, by the figure of a naked American Indian with his ear to the ground, a bow and arrow in his hand, and a look of special knowledge in his eyes."

It was Arthur Schopenhauer, the philosopher whose writings would later greatly influence Campbell, who observed that

> the experiences and illuminations of childhood and early youth become in later life the types, standards and patterns of all subsequent knowledge and experience, or as it were, the categories according to which all later things are classified—not always consciously, however. And so it is that in our childhood years the foundation is laid

of our later view of the world, and therewith as well of its superficiality or depth: it will be in later years unfolded and fulfilled, not essentially changed.

And so it was with young Joseph Campbell. Even as he actively practiced (until well into his twenties) the faith of his forebears, he became consumed with Native American culture; and his worldview was arguably shaped by the dynamic tension between these two mythological perspectives. On the one hand, he was immersed in the rituals, symbols, and rich traditions of his Irish Catholic heritage; on the other, he was obsessed with primitive (or, as he later preferred, "primal") people's direct experience of what he came to describe as "the continuously created dynamic display of an absolutely transcendent, yet universally immanent, *mysterium tremendum et fascinans,* which is the ground at once of the whole spectacle and of oneself."*

By the age of ten, Joe had read every book on American Indians in the children's section of his local library and was admitted to the adult stacks, where he eventually read the entire multivolume *Reports of the Bureau of American Ethnology.* He worked on wampum belts, started his own "tribe" (the "Lenni-Lenape"), and frequented the American Museum of Natural History, where he became fascinated with totem poles and masks, thus beginning a lifelong exploration of that museum's vast collection.

After spending much of his thirteenth year recuperating from a respiratory illness, Joe briefly attended Iona, a private school in Westchester, New York, before his mother enrolled him at Canterbury, a Catholic residential school in New Milford, Connecticut. His high school years were rich and rewarding, though marked by a major tragedy: in 1919, the Campbell home was consumed by a fire that killed his grandmother and destroyed all of the family's possessions.

Joe graduated from Canterbury in 1921, and the following September entered Dartmouth College; but he was soon disillusioned with the social scene and disappointed by a lack of academic rigor, so he transferred to Columbia University, where he excelled: while specializing in medieval literature, he played in a jazz band and became a star runner. In 1924, while on a steamship journey to Europe with his family, Joe met and befriended Jiddu Krishnamurti, the young messiah-elect of the Theosophical Society,

---

* Campbell, *The Historical Atlas of World Mythology,* vol. 1, pt. 1, p. 8.

thus beginning a friendship that would be renewed intermittently over the next five years.

After earning a B.A. from Columbia (1925) and receiving an M.A. (1927) for his work in Arthurian studies, Joe was awarded a Proudfit Traveling Fellowship to continue his studies at the University of Paris (1927–28). Then, after he had received and rejected an offer to teach at his high school alma mater, his fellowship was renewed, and he traveled to Germany to resume his studies at the University of Munich (1928–29).

It was during this period in Europe that Joe was first exposed to those modernist masters—notably, the sculptor Antoine Bourdelle, Pablo Picasso, Paul Klee, James Joyce, Thomas Mann, Sigmund Freud, and Carl Jung—whose art and insights would greatly influence his own work. These encounters would eventually lead him to theorize that all myths are the creative products of the human psyche, that artists are a culture's myth-makers, and that mythologies are creative manifestations of humankind's universal need to explain psychological, social, cosmological, and spiritual realities.

When Joe returned from Europe late in August of 1929, he was at a crossroads, unable to decide what to do with his life. With the onset of the Great Depression, he found himself with no hope of obtaining a teaching job, and so he spent most of the next two years reconnecting with his family, reading, renewing old acquaintances, and writing copious entries in his journal. Then, late in 1931, after exploring and rejecting the possibility of a doctoral program or teaching job at Columbia, he decided, like countless young men before and since, to "hit the road," to undertake a cross-country journey in which he hoped to experience "the soul of America" and, in the process, perhaps discover the purpose of his life. In January of 1932, when he was leaving Los Angeles, where he had been studying Russian in order to read *War and Peace* in the vernacular, he pondered his future in this journal entry:

> I begin to think that I have a genius for working like an ox over to-
> tally irrelevant subjects. . . . I am filled with an excruciating sense of
> never having gotten anywhere—but when I sit down and try to dis-
> cover where it is I want to get, I'm at a loss. . . . The thought of grow-
> ing into a professor gives me the creeps. A lifetime to be spent trying
> to kid myself and my pupils into believing that the thing that we are

looking for is in books! I don't know where it is—but I feel just now pretty sure that it isn't in books—It isn't in travel.—It isn't in California.—It isn't in New York....Where is it? And what is it, after all?

Thus one real result of my Los Angeles stay was the elimination of Anthropology from the running. I suddenly realized that all of my primitive and American Indian excitement might easily be incorporated in a literary career.—I am convinced now that no field but that of English literature would have permitted me the almost unlimited roaming about from this to that which I have been enjoying. A science would buckle me down—and would probably yield no more important fruit than literature may yield me!—If I want to justify my existence, and continue to be obsessed with the notion that I've got to do something for humanity—well, teaching ought to quell that obsession—and if I can ever get around to an intelligent view of matters, intelligent criticism of contemporary values ought to be useful to the world. This gets back again to Krishna's dictum: The best way to help mankind is through the perfection of yourself.

His travels next carried him north to San Francisco, then back south to Pacific Grove, where he spent the better part of a year in the company of Carol and John Steinbeck and marine biologist Ed Ricketts. During this time, he wrestled with his writing, discovered the poems of Robinson Jeffers, first read Oswald Spengler's *Decline of the West,* and wrote to some seventy colleges and universities in an unsuccessful attempt to secure employment. Finally, he was offered a teaching position at the Canterbury School. He returned to the East Coast, where he endured an unhappy year as a Canterbury housemaster, the one bright moment being when he sold his first short story ("Strictly Platonic") to *Liberty* magazine. Then, in 1933, he moved to a cottage without running water on Maverick Road in Woodstock, New York, where he spent a year reading and writing. In 1934, he was offered and accepted a position in the literature department at Sarah Lawrence College, a post he would retain for thirty-eight years.

In 1938, he married one of his students, Jean Erdman, who would become a major presence in the emerging field of modern dance, first as a star dancer in Martha Graham's fledgling troupe and later as dancer/choreographer of her own company.

Even as he continued his teaching career, Joe's life continued to unfold serendipitously. In 1940, he was introduced to Swami Nikhilananda, who enlisted his help in producing a new translation of *The Gospel of Sri Ramakrishna.* Subsequently, Nikhilananda introduced Joe to the Indologist Heinrich Zimmer, who introduced him to a member of the editorial board at the Bollingen Foundation. Bollingen, which had been founded by Paul and Mary Mellon to "develop scholarship and research in the liberal arts and sciences and other fields of cultural endeavor generally," was embarking upon an ambitious publishing project, the Bollingen Series. Joe was invited to contribute an "Introduction and Commentary" to the first Bollingen publication, *Where the Two Came to Their Father: A Navaho War Ceremonial.*

When Zimmer died unexpectedly in 1943 at the age of fifty-two, his widow, Christiana, and Mary Mellon asked Joe to oversee the publication of his unfinished works. Joe would eventually edit and complete four volumes from Zimmer's posthumous papers: *Myths and Symbols in Indian Art and Civilization, The King and the Corpse, Philosophies of India,* and a two-volume opus, *The Art of Indian Asia.*

Joe, meanwhile, followed his initial Bollingen contribution with a "Folkloristic Commentary" to *Grimm's Fairy Tales;* he also coauthored (with Henry Morton Robinson) *A Skeleton Key to Finnegans Wake,* the first major study of James Joyce's notoriously complex novel.

His first full-length solo authorial endeavor, *The Hero with a Thousand Faces,* was published to acclaim and brought him the first of numerous awards and honors, the National Institute of Arts and Letters Award for Contributions to Creative Literature. In this study of the myth of the hero, Campbell posits the existence of a monomyth (a word he borrowed from James Joyce), a universal pattern that is the essence of, and common to, heroic tales in every culture. While outlining the basic stages of this mythic cycle, he also explores common variations in the hero's journey, which, he argues, is an operative metaphor not only for an individual but for a culture as well. *The Hero* would prove to have a major influence on generations of creative artists—from the Abstract Expressionists in the 1950s to contemporary filmmakers today—and would, in time, come to be acclaimed as a classic.

Joe would eventually author dozens of articles and numerous other books, including *The Masks of God: Primitive Mythology, Oriental Mythology, Occidental Mythology,* and *Creative Mythology; The Flight of the Wild Gander: Explorations in the Mythological Dimension; Myths to Live By; The Mythic Image; The Inner Reaches of Outer Space: Metaphor as Myth and as Religion;* and five books in his four-volume, multipart, unfinished *Historical Atlas of World Mythology.*

He was also a prolific editor. Over the years, he edited *The Portable Arabian Nights* and was general editor of the series *Man and Myth,* which included major works by Maya Deren *(Divine Horsemen: The Living Gods of Haiti),* Carl Kerenyi *(The Gods of the Greeks),* and Alan Watts *(Myth and Ritual in Christianity).* He also edited *The Portable Jung,* as well as six volumes of *Papers from the Eranos Yearbooks: Spirit and Nature, The Mysteries, Man and Time, Spiritual Disciplines, Man and Transformation,* and *The Mystic Vision.*

His many publications notwithstanding, it was arguably as a public speaker that Joe had his greatest popular impact. From the time of his first public lecture in 1940—a talk at the Ramakrishna-Vivekananda Center entitled "Sri Ramakrishna's Message to the West"—it was apparent that he was an erudite but accessible lecturer, a gifted storyteller, and a witty raconteur. In the ensuing years, he was asked more and more often to speak at different venues on various topics. In 1956, he was invited to speak at the State Department's Foreign Service Institute; working without notes, he delivered two straight days of lectures. His talks were so well received, he was invited back annually for the next seventeen years. In the mid-1950s, he also undertook a series of public lectures at Cooper Union in New York City; these talks drew an ever-larger, increasingly diverse audience and soon became a regular event.

Joe first lectured at Esalen Institute in 1965. Each year thereafter, he returned to Big Sur to share his latest thoughts, insights, and stories. And as the years passed, he came to look forward more and more to his annual sojourns to the place he called "paradise on the Pacific Coast." Although he retired from teaching at Sarah Lawrence in 1972 to devote himself to his writing, he continued to undertake two monthlong lecture tours each year.

In 1985, Joe was awarded the National Arts Club Gold Medal of Honor in Literature. At the award ceremony, James Hillman remarked, "No one in our century—not Freud, not Thomas Mann, not Lévi-Strauss

—has so brought the mythical sense of the world and its eternal figures back into our everyday consciousness."

Joseph Campbell died unexpectedly in 1987 after a brief struggle with cancer. In 1988, millions were introduced to his ideas by the broadcast on PBS of *Joseph Campbell and the Power of Myth with Bill Moyers,* six hours of an electrifying conversation that the two men had videotaped over the course of several years. When he died, *Newsweek* magazine noted that "Campbell has become one of the rarest of intellectuals in American life: a serious thinker who has been embraced by the popular culture."

In his later years, Joe was fond of recalling how Schopenhauer, in his essay "On the Apparent Intention in the Fate of the Individual," wrote of the curious feeling one can have of there being an author somewhere writing the novel of our lives, in such a way that through events that seem to us to be chance happenings there is actually a plot unfolding of which we have no knowledge.

Looking back over Joe's life, one cannot help but feel that it proves the truth of Schopenhauer's observation.

ABOUT THE
JOSEPH CAMPBELL FOUNDATION

THE JOSEPH CAMPBELL FOUNDATION (JCF) is a nonprofit corporation that continues the work of Joseph Campbell, exploring the fields of mythology and comparative religion. The Foundation is guided by three principal goals:

First, the Foundation preserves, protects, and perpetuates Campbell's pioneering work. This includes cataloging and archiving his works, developing new publications based on his works, directing the sale and distribution of his published works, protecting copyrights to his works, and increasing awareness of his works by making them available in digital formats on JCF's Web site.

Second, the Foundation promotes the study of mythology and comparative religion. This involves implementing and/or supporting diverse mythological education programs, supporting and/or sponsoring events designed to increase public awareness, donating Campbell's archived works (principally to the Joseph Campbell and Marija Gimbutas Archive and Library), and utilizing JCF's Web site as a forum for relevant cross-cultural dialogue.

Third, the Foundation helps individuals enrich their lives by participating in a series of programs, including our global, Internet-based Associates program, our local international network of Mythological Roundtables, and our periodic Joseph Campbell–related events and activities.

For more information on Joseph Campbell
and the Joseph Campbell Foundation, contact:

JOSEPH CAMPBELL FOUNDATION
www.jcf.org
Post Office Box 36
San Anselmo, CA 94979-0036
Toll free: (800) 330-MYTH
E-mail: info@jcf.org